Israel at the Polls 2013

The 2013 elections took place less than two years after the overwhelming wave of social protests of summer 2011. At first, the election campaign did not raise much public interest, but the emergence of new players and young political forces energized the political race. Polls conducted throughout the campaign greatly deviated from the final results, which eventually enabled Prime Minister Benjamin Netanyahu to form a cabinet again, despite a loss of 11 seats for his list.

This book describes and analyses a variety of political and sociological developments in Israel both before and after the elections. These include the nature of the campaign, the developments in the National Camp, among religious Zionists, the ultra-Orthodox parties, and the Russian vote. Furthermore, it assesses the impact of media, including new media.

The variety of subjects makes the book suitable for undergraduate and graduate students in Middle-Eastern, Israeli, and Jewish studies, as well as political science and liberal arts in general. *Israel at the Polls* has been updated and published regularly for thirty-five years, providing readers with up-to-date analysis and continuity of scholarship. This book offers a long-term assessment of Israeli politics.

This book was published as a special issue of *Israel Affairs*.

Eithan Orkibi is a lecturer in the Department of Sociology and Anthropology at Ariel University, and a member of the ADARR (Analysis of Discourse, Argumentation and Rhetoric) research group, Tel Aviv. He specializes in political culture, discourse analysis and persuasive communication.

Manfred Gerstenfeld is the Emeritus Chairman of the Jerusalem Center for Public Affairs, Israel. He is the former editor of The Jewish Political Studies Review, and has published twenty-three books covering diverse areas such as anti-Semitism, Judaism and the environment, contemporary history, and Jewish public affairs.

Israel at the Polls 2013

Continuity and change in Israeli
political culture

Edited by
Eithan Orkibi and Manfred Gerstenfeld

Routledge
Taylor & Francis Group

LONDON AND NEW YORK

First published 2016
by Routledge
2 Park Square, Milton Park, Abingdon, Oxon, OX14 4RN, UK

and by Routledge
711 Third Avenue, New York, NY 10017, USA

First issued in paperback 2017

Routledge is an imprint of the Taylor & Francis Group, an informa business

British Library Cataloguing in Publication Data
A catalogue record for this book is available from the British Library

ISBN 13: 978-1-138-20459-1 (pbk)
ISBN 13: 978-1-138-94587-6 (hbk)

Typeset in Times New Roman
by RefineCatch Limited, Bungay, Suffolk

Publisher's Note
The publisher accepts responsibility for any inconsistencies that may have
arisen during the conversion of this book from journal articles to book chapters,
namely the possible inclusion of journal terminology.

Disclaimer
Every effort has been made to contact copyright holders for their permission to
reprint material in this book. The publishers would be grateful to hear from any
copyright holder who is not here acknowledged and will undertake to rectify
any errors or omissions in future editions of this book.

Contents

Citation Information

The chapters in this book were originally published in *Israel Affairs*, volume 21, issue 2 (April 2015). When citing this material, please use the original page numbering for each article, as follows:

Chapter 1
The Run-Up to Israel's 2013 Elections: A Political History
Manfred Gerstenfeld
Israel Affairs, volume 21, issue 2 (April 2015) pp. 177–194

Chapter 2
The Peculiar Victory of The National Camp in the 2013 Israeli Election
Arie Perliger and Eran Zaidise
Israel Affairs, volume 21, issue 2 (April 2015) pp. 195–208

Chapter 3
'Something new begins' – religious Zionism in the 2013 elections: from decline to political recovery
Anat Roth
Israel Affairs, volume 21, issue 2 (April 2015) pp. 209–229

Chapter 4
An uneasy stability: the Haredi parties' emergency campaign for the 2013 elections
Nissim Leon
Israel Affairs, volume 21, issue 2 (April 2015) pp. 230–244

Chapter 5
The political transformation of the Israeli 'Russian' street in the 2013 elections
Vladimir (Ze'ev) Khanin
Israel Affairs, volume 21, issue 2 (April 2015) pp. 245–261

Chapter 6

The Transmigration of Media Personalities and Celebrities to Politics: The Case of Yair Lapid
Rafi Mann
Israel Affairs, volume 21, issue 2 (April 2015) pp. 262–276

Chapter 7

'New politics', new media – new political language? A rhetorical perspective on candidates' self-presentation in electronic campaigns in the 2013 Israeli elections
Eithan Orkibi
Israel Affairs, volume 21, issue 2 (April 2015) pp. 277–292

Chapter 8

The 2013 Israeli elections and historic recurrences
Eyal Lewin
Israel Affairs, volume 21, issue 2 (April 2015) pp. 293–308

For any permission-related enquiries please visit:
http://www.tandfonline.com/page/help/permissions

The Run-Up to Israel's 2013 Elections: A Political History

Manfred Gerstenfeld

Jerusalem Center for Public Affairs, Jerusalem, Israel

On 15 October 2012, the 18th Knesset – which had been elected in February 2009 – voted unanimously to dissolve. The date for the elections for the 19th Knesset was then set for 22 January 2013. This article follows the events leading to the election day. It shows that there were four distinct phases during that period. It describes the internal organization and primary elections in Israel's major parties, Likud and Avoda; the debate about the formation of political alliances which led to the joint list of Likud–Israel Beiteinu; the stabilization of the political blocs; and the emergence of new political forces (such as Yesh Atid). The article also discusses the impact of major events, such as the military operation Pillar of Defence, on the elections and the electoral campaign. The article discusses the parties' campaigns and the proliferation of opinion polls. It also shows that much of the campaigning of the parties was directed against other parties of the same bloc, be it the centre-right or the centre-left.

On 15 October 2012, the 18th Knesset – which had been elected in February 2009 – voted unanimously to dissolve. The date for the elections for the 19th Knesset was then set for 22 January 2013. Prime Minister Benjamin Netanyahu said that the Knesset had to be dissolved as he could not obtain a majority for his proposed budget.[1]

The first few weeks thereafter were characterized by several significant manoeuvres. There were initial efforts to build a centre-left mega-party led by former Prime Minister Ehud Olmert. It was to include his two successors at the head of the Kadima party, Tzipi Livni and then leader Shaul Mofaz, as well as political newcomer Yair Lapid. The latter, a well-known media figure, founded a new party, Yesh Atid (There is a Future). A *Jerusalem Post* poll gave the theoretical mega-party 31 seats. It found that the Likud, which held 27 seats in the outgoing Knesset, would only receive 22 seats.[2]

Olmert began to consider the possibility of his return to politics. He had resigned in 2008 in light of corruption allegations against him.[3] In September 2012, he was the first Israeli Prime Minister to be convicted by a court, which found him guilty of a lesser offence, breach of trust. This conviction did not include moral turpitude, which would have prevented him from running for the Knesset. Yet he remained under investigation in another trial concerning bribery by real estate developers.[4] Later the State Prosecutor appealed Olmert's acquittal.[5]

Sources close to Livni said that she was considering returning to politics as the head of a new party.[6] An Israel Radio poll on 30 October found that Labour Party leader, Shelly Yachimovich, was the preferred leader of the centre-left, well ahead of Olmert, Livni, Mofaz and Lapid.[7] A number of polls followed each other, some of which included various hypothetical situations for the centre-left and arrived at greatly varying results.

The many assumptions on new possibilities in the centre-left derived from the crumbling of almost all support for Kadima. In 2009 it had won 28 seats to become the largest party ahead of the Likud. Kadima had joined the Netanyahu government in May 2012, thus preventing early elections. However in July, as Netanyahu was unwilling to introduce full conscription for ultra-Orthodox recruits, Kadima left the government again.[8]

The joint Likud/Yisrael Beiteinu list

The major surprises, however, came from the right of the political spectrum. Netanyahu and Foreign Minister Avigdor Lieberman, leader of Yisrael Beiteinu (Israel is our Home), which held 15 seats, announced that they had agreed to run on a combined ticket. A few days later, both parties approved it. Some interpreted it as a panic reaction by Netanyahu to the centre-left discussion about establishing a party which would win more seats than Likud. Others saw it as Netanyahu assuring himself that the centre-right bloc would most probably form the next government and return him as Prime Minister.

For Lieberman, being number two on the combined list if the two parties were to merge later could have brought him closer to his long-term aim of becoming Prime Minister. Their American adviser, Arthur Finkelstein, had forecast that the combined list would receive 45 seats against the 42 they held jointly. Yet Israeli experience has shown that party mergers often lead to fewer mandates than if the components run separately. After their announcement, one poll indicated a loss of four seats.[9] Things only went downhill from there.

Popular Likud Minister of Communications Moshe Kahlon initially declared that he would not be a candidate in the next elections. Thereafter, he toyed for a few days with the idea of establishing a new party which would highlight social issues. Polls gave him 10 or more seats.[10]

When he announced a few days later that he had abandoned his plans, there was relief both in the Likud and in the ultra-Orthodox Shas party which also focuses on social issues. Shas had closed ranks when it brought back its former leader Aryeh Deri. He would become number two on its list, behind party chairman Eli Yishai.[11] Ten years after ending his prison term on bribery charges, Deri was legally allowed to return to politics.

Other developments concerned the entrance of new candidates into various parties. Yachimovich considered that Labour needed more 'visible' candidates and wanted to reduce the party's reserved seats for various sectors. She seemingly solved the problem by bringing in General Uri Saguy, a former military intelligence chief.[12] He withdrew his candidacy shortly thereafter. Several Kadima parliamentarians and senior politicians jumped ship to join the Likud or Labour.

A number of polls indicated that the Independence Party of Defence Minister Ehud Barak might just pass the threshold, or might fail.[13] They also raised doubts as to whether Kadima would receive enough votes to pass the threshold.[14] This indicated already what on election day would become the most dramatic fall in Israeli parliamentary history.

Operation Pillar of Defence

On 14 November the eight-day-long Operation Pillar of Defence battle against Hamas in Gaza began. That could be considered the end of the first phase of the election campaign. By far the most important development in the first month of campaigning had been the decision to form the joint Likud/Yisrael Beiteinu list.

Some smaller parties had already held their primaries. The extremely dovish Meretz party put its three sitting MKs at the top of its list, headed by party leader Zahava Gal-On.[15] Among religious Zionists, Habayit Hayehudi chose newcomer Naftali Bennett as its head. He defeated veteran politician Zevulun Orlev, who thereafter left politics. A few days later, candidates for its Knesset list were elected.[16] The party merged with the Tekuma faction of the National Union, which chose sitting MK Uri Ariel as its leader.[17] On the extreme right, Michael Ben Ari and Aryeh Eldad broke away from the National Union to form a new party, Otzma Leyisrael (Strong Israel).[18]

On the centre-left confusion still reigned when Operation Pillar of Defence started. At one point Livni even suggested that 89-year-old President Shimon Peres resign and run for the Knesset to try to beat Netanyahu as Prime Minister.[19]

Operation Pillar of Defence gained wide support among the Israeli population. On its first day, three different polls found between 84% and 91% in its favour.[20] Mofaz,[21] Yachimovich and Lapid backed the operation. Gal-On opposed it, claiming that it would not help the situation.[22] Hanin Zoabi of the Arab Balad party called Pillar of Defence 'a hostile war against the Palestinian people'. Before voting in their party's primaries Balad members observed a moment of silence for the Palestinians killed in the Israeli strikes on Gaza.[23]

Phase two: After Pillar of Defence

During Operation Pillar of Defence, the election battle was on a back-burner. The 21 November ceasefire with Hamas garnered mixed support in Israeli opinion.

A poll found that 49% of Israelis opposed ending the battle without a ground invasion.[24] There was harsh criticism of the government from right-wing politicians for ending the operation.

Opinion polls held immediately after the end of Pillar of Defence showed marked differences from the previous ones. A Panels Research poll found a substantial further decline of the Likud/Yisrael Beiteinu list. It would get only 33 seats. Labour would receive 24 seats, while the Habayit Hayehudi list was projected to have 13 MKs. Otzmah Leyisrael was predicted to pass the election threshold with four seats.[25]

Livni now indicated that she might enter the fray with a new list. A Channel Two poll then gave Likud/Yisrael Beiteinu 38 seats. Livni's new list would get nine seats and the list headed by Lapid four seats.[26] Yachimovich urged Livni to join Labour.[27] Lapid offered Livni the second place on his list.[28]

Before previous elections, there had been unsuccessful attempts to exclude some of the Arab lists. This time Likud MK Danny Danon asked the elections committee to ban Zoabi from running. He also initiated a petition to this effect, signed by 50,000 people.[29]

Likud and Labour primaries

Eyes then turned toward the Likud primaries on 25 November. Major computer problems resulted in an extension of voting for another day. About 80,000 Likud members put a rather hawkish list in place. The first 20 positions on the Likud list, which were chosen nationally, returned 18 sitting MKs.[30] Right-winger Moshe Feiglin obtained a safe spot after several unsuccessful past attempts. Veteran ministers Benny Begin, Dan Meridor and Michael Eitan did not succeed in winning realistic positions. Nor did Internal Security Minister Avi Dichter, who had come over from Kadima.[31]

On 26 November, Defence Minister Ehud Barak, leader of the Independence party announced he was quitting politics.[32] Its MK Einat Wilf made it known that Barak was trying to convince Minister Dan Meridor to take over the party's leadership after he had failed to secure a safe spot in the Likud primaries. She said that a poll showed that Independence would then win 10–11 seats.[33] After Meridor rejected the offer, the party decided not to participate in the elections.[34]

On 27 November, Livni officially announced that she would head a new party, Hatnuah (The Movement).[35] With this announcement it became clear who the main parties participating in the elections would be.

The Labour primaries gave many safe spots to newcomers. After Barak had split off in 2011 with four other MKs to form the Independence party, Labour only had eight seats left. Former Minister Isaac Herzog, an ally of Yachimovich, beat former party leader Amir Peretz for the second spot on the list.[36]

Yisrael Beiteinu's list of candidates had only one newcomer in its top 10: senior businessman Yair Shamir in the second spot. Surprisingly, Deputy Foreign Minister Danny Ayalon was left off the list.[37]

Yesh Atid brought in as its most visible newcomer former domestic intelligence chief Yaakov Perry, who also had a successful business career.[38] Former Labour party leader Amram Mitzna joined Livni. Like Peretz, he was defeated in the 2011 elections for the Labour leadership by Yachimovich. Livni had persuaded seven MKs from Kadima to join Hatnuah. This faction split meant state pre-election financing of more than 5 million shekels as well as greatly increased campaign broadcasting time.[39]

The end of the second phase

On 6 December, the second phase of the election campaign ended with the submission of the party lists.[40] Its main events had been the establishment of lists of candidates by the parties, as well as the splintering of the centre-left. The last day brought a major surprise. Peretz gave his third place on the Labour list up for the same one with Hatnuah. His relationship with Labour leader Shelly Yachimovich had turned increasingly sour.[41]

Almost all polls at the time showed that Likud/Yisrael Beiteinu together with the national-religious and ultra-Orthodox parties would together gain between 65 and 70 seats. The Arab parties polled at around 10 seats.

This left approximately 40–45 seats for which the centre-left parties could compete. After the lists were submitted, a *Maariv* poll gave Labour 18 seats, Hatnuah 10 and Yesh Atid five.[42]

The third phase

After the party's lists had been submitted the campaign intensified. In the 2009 elections there had been a fierce battle for the premiership between Netanyahu and Livni, with then-Labour leader Barak claiming that he was also in the running. This time a poll found that 81% of Israelis were convinced that Benjamin Netanyahu would continue as Prime Minister after the elections.[43] This may have accounted for much of the subdued public interest in the campaign. The absence of both a true leadership contest and a central theme gave a somewhat anaemic character to the 2013 election campaign.

This would last for most of the remaining time. The government announced various activities, including new settlement plans. The opposition criticized them and many politicians made statements on a variety of issues. The general public did not seem to care much.

Lieberman indicted

On 13 December Attorney General Yehuda Weinstein announced that he would indict Foreign Minister Lieberman on charges of breach of trust and fraud. However, the main case against him concerning money laundering and much wider fraud was closed. It had been investigated for 12 years. When Lieberman's indictment became known, the opposition parties called for his immediate resignation. He did so the next day. Thus there was little opposition mileage left on this issue.[44]

Bennett caused a commotion when he stated that he would refuse an order to expel Jews from their homes. He was severely criticized by both the Likud and the opposition parties. Thereupon he retreated by saying: 'As someone who led fighters into operations many times, I am opposed with all my heart and soul to refusing an order. I fulfilled all the orders I received in my 22 years in the IDF and will continue to do so.'[45]

The Central Elections Committee decided to ban Arab extremist MK Hanin Zoabi of Balad from participating in the elections. This decision was automatically referred to the Supreme Court.[46] The court would later unanimously overturn the Central Elections Committee's decision, so that Zoabi could be a candidate. The Likud reacted, saying that the existing law which made this court decision possible should be changed.[47]

Discouragement from the Egyptian and Palestinian side

Events on the Egyptian and Palestinian side did not encourage parties of the centre-left to claim that Israel could foster peace by making further concessions to the Palestinians. In October, a video had been posted of Egyptian President Mohammed Morsi answering 'Amen' to a praying imam who asked Allah to destroy the Jews.[48] It also became known that in 2010, Morsi said that there would be no negotiations with 'the sons of apes and pigs'.[49] This was a reference to the Koran, which describes Jews in this insulting way.

Early in December Hamas Leader Khaled Mashaal visited Gaza for the first time in 40 years. He reiterated that his movement aimed at destroying Israel. Mashaal said: 'Today is Gaza, tomorrow will be Ramalla and after that Jerusalem, then Haifa and Jaffa.'[50]

Less than two weeks later a poll conducted by the Palestinian Centre for Policy and Survey Research showed that 48% of Palestinians would have voted for Ismail Haniyeh, the Hamas Prime Minister in Gaza, as Palestinian President. He would defeat the incumbent Mahmoud Abbas, who would get 45% of the votes.[51]

There were many foreign condemnations of the government's announced building plans in the Occupied Territories.[52] The Israeli public, which watches these statements vis-à-vis the subdued international criticism of mass murders and many other atrocities in Muslim countries, did not seem impressed.

No crossing over between blocs

Polls continued to show that voters within the centre-right and centre-left were not considering crossing over between the blocs. A Smith poll gave Likud/ Yisrael Beiteinu only 36 seats. Habayit Hayehudi was increasing in strength with 11 seats. On the centre-left side, Labour with 19 seats remained ahead of Yesh Atid with 11 and Hatnuah with nine.[53] The poll seemed to confirm earlier indications that the electoral battle would be mainly inside the various blocs.

Initially, the Likud/Yisrael Beiteinu campaign focused its attacks on the centre-left parties. It now decided to increase its attacks against Habayit Hayehudi, to which it seemed to be losing many votes.[54] Likud spokesmen, like those of the centre-left parties, strongly attacked Bennett when he said that he would rather go to jail than expel Jews from their homes. This even after he had quickly backtracked.[55] Netanyahu stated that he would not admit refusal advocates into his government.[56]

The Likud's strategy backfired. It propelled Bennett into a central position in the lack-lustre campaign. Likud/Yisrael Beiteinu was even fined for sponsoring anonymous anti-Bennett ads.[57] Feiglin criticized his party's advisors and forecast that their joint list would lose votes to Habayit Hayehudi. This was confirmed by all polls.[58]

A poll showed that one-third of those intending to vote for Habayit Hayehudi defined themselves as secular, while 40% of its votes came from people under the age of 30.[59] After Bennett's retracted statement, some voices within the Likud were heard saying that refusing orders to expel Jews is the right thing to do. An emboldened Bennett asked Netanyahu to abandon his support for a two-state solution.[60]

The centre-left parties had hoped that social issues would be a predominant factor in the campaign. In 2011 there had been huge street demonstrations against the government on these matters. Yet focusing on these issues seemed to serve only to draw votes from other parties within the same bloc.

There were polls on other issues as well. A Dahaf poll for the Jerusalem Centre for Public Affairs showed that 83% of Jewish voters did not believe that an Israeli withdrawal to the 1967 lines and a division of Jerusalem would end the Israeli–Palestinian conflict. Seventy-eight per cent of Jews said they would vote differently if the party they supported stated that it was prepared to relinquish sovereignty in East Jerusalem.[61] These data showed that security was more of an issue for many than a possible peace process.

A harsher indictment for Lieberman

Toward the end of the year, the Attorney General presented the Knesset with an updated more severe indictment of fraud and breach of trust against Lieberman.[62] He had kept a low profile in the campaign in view of the earlier indictment. Yet Lieberman announced that he would, in the next Knesset, chair the Foreign Affairs Committee until his acquittal.[63]

The partial vacuum created by the merged Likud/Israel Beiteinu list and Lieberman's inability to play a major role in the campaign gave Bennett the opportunity to position Habayit Hayehudi firmly to the right of Netanyahu.

He remained in the news by accusing Netanyahu of wanting to form a government after the elections with Hatnuah and Yesh Atid.[64]

With Netanyahu's likely return as Prime Minister, rumours with respect to the composition of the next government multiplied. Deri stated that Shas again saw itself as a natural partner in a future Netanyahu government.[65] There were persistent rumours that Livni had approached Netanyahu about joining the next government and becoming Foreign Minister.[66] Negative reactions in his party led Netanyahu to state that he was reserving that ministry for Lieberman and that he disagreed with Livni's policies.[67]

Yachimovich challenged Netanyahu to a televised debate.[68] This move underlined that the Labour leader viewed herself as the leader of the centre-left. She kept stressing social issues as her party's main concern. To avoid accusations that Labour had abandoned its traditional values, Yachimovich added that peace negotiations with the Palestinians should be renewed.[69]

Livni promoted the idea that peace could be achieved through negotiations. Lapid positioned himself as spokesman of the middle class, saying: 'We will not allow the ongoing abuse of the productive, army serving, educated and working citizen to continue.' He said that raising taxes was his party's red line.[70]

Likud Finance Minister Yuval Steinitz declared that no substantial tax hikes were planned for 2013. The Governor of the Bank of Israel, Stanley Fischer, thereupon stated publicly that tax increases *were* needed.[71] Yet none of this raised much interest.

Sniping dominates

At the beginning of the new year polls indicated that Likud/Israel Beiteinu could lose up to 10 seats.[72] Its candidates made contradictory statements. Netanyahu repeated that he was in favour of a 'two-state solution'.[73] Lieberman did the same.[74] However, two Likud candidates, Minister Yuri Edelstein and MK Zeev Elkin, called for annexing Area C of the West Bank which is presently under Israeli military control. Jews account for the great majority of the residents there.[75]

Later Likud Deputy Prime Minister Moshe Ya'alon spoke out against establishing a Palestinian state next to Israel.[76] Yair Shamir – number four on the combined list – said that 'Netanyahu is zigzagging because he wants to please his voters'.[77] When he was criticized thereafter, Shamir claimed that he had been misunderstood.[78]

Yet due to the absence of both a leadership contest and a central controversial issue, the campaign continued to be characterized by sniping between the parties and their leaders. Part of the fragmented debate, however, was largely hidden as it took place through social media.

Egyptian and Palestinian leaders continued to impress upon Israelis that they were aiming for Israel's destruction rather than peace. Morsi associate Essam el-Erian, Deputy Head of the Muslim Brotherhood's Freedom and Justice Party, stated publicly that Israel would cease to exist within 10 years.[79]

Hamas leaders invented a new game plan besides repeating that Israel has to be destroyed. They told Palestinian President Mahmoud Abbas that they were willing to take over rule of the West Bank.[80] On the Israeli side, Shimon Peres – who as President is not supposed to express personal opinions on controversial political issues – told a gathering of Israeli ambassadors that Abbas is 'a partner for peace'.[81]

Feiglin was arrested for attempting to pray out loud on the Temple Mount. It was the third time that he has been detained for similar offences.[82] He also tried to raise attention with statements such as that Palestinians should be offered financial incentives to emigrate from the West Bank.[83]

The Likud faced internal dissent regarding its negative campaign against Bennett.[84] Several important supporters argued that it should focus its attacks on opposition parties of the centre-left instead.[85] In addition to attacking Bennett, the Likud began to proclaim that if it lost any seats, the post-election government would not be able to pass necessary political measures.

Deri was trying to resurrect his public image by making controversial statements about where Shas was positioned on the political map[86] and what its future demands for ministries would be.[87] He also tried to revive the ethnic issue, stating that the Likud/Israel Beiteinu was a party of 'whites and Russians', He quickly apologized, yet then stated that Netanyahu would not appoint senior Sephardic ministers.[88]

Positioning on the centre-left

Opposition parties of the centre-left did not seem to gain much from the disarray in Likud/Israel Beiteinu. Polls still did not show any movement of voters from the centre-right to the centre-left. Yachimovich thereupon changed strategy and said that she would either form the next government, or lead the opposition.[89] By positioning herself in that way, she apparently hoped to draw votes away from Hatnuah and Yesh Atid. Lapid announced that his party would not enter a government which was solely composed of right-wing and religious parties.[90]

As election day drew closer, the inter-party sniping increased. A few examples: Minister Steinitz said that Labour would make Israel's economy similar to Spain's.[91] Lapid said that Livni would leave the Knesset if she did not get enough mandates.[92] His party also claimed that Yachimovich was in a 'hysterical fit'.[93] In the meantime, however, leading parties were left searching for a major campaign issue to carry them over until election day.

On 6 January, at Livni's initiative, she met with Yachimovich and Lapid to discuss forming a unified bloc to challenge Netanyahu. No agreement was reached however. When Livni said thereafter that her proposals were refused by the other two, Yachimovich and Lapid jointly retorted that she was misrepresenting the meeting's content. Their statement included: 'It is now clear that the invitation to a three-way meeting was merely a ploy perpetrated by Livni, who is in despair over her falling poll numbers.'[94]

One major news development that week was the State Comptroller's report on the forged document produced by reserve officer Lt. Col. Boaz Harpaz. He had tried to prevent the appointment of General Yoav Galant as Chief of Staff. Defence Minister Ehud Barak was one of those criticized in the report.[95] Yet as Barak was not up for re-election in the Knesset, it could not be turned into a relevant campaign issue.

The fourth phase: election broadcasting

The campaign thereafter moved into its fourth and final phase with the start of the advertising campaigns on television and radio on 8 January. The main issues at stake seemed to be whether the Likud/Yisrael Beiteinu could halt its decline in the polls, whether Habayit Hayehudi would be able to maintain its strong position and how voters would choose between the centre-left parties. Less than two weeks before the election date, polls indicated that undecided voters still represented around 25% of the electorate.[96] Thus true support for the various parties remained uncertain.

The parties were mainly concentrating on frequent repetition of their key messages. Likud/Yisrael Beiteinu focused its campaign on two main issues. One was the achievements of Prime Minister Binyamin Netanyahu's government. It stressed the government's economic performance, the creation of 350,000 jobs, the revolution in the cellular telephone market and the wall built on the Egyptian border to stop the influx of economic immigrants from Africa. The advertisements also showed Netanyahu's address in the US Congress, during which he received several standing ovations. This illustrated their message that when Netanyahu speaks, the world listens.

Likud/Yisrael Beiteinu's second important broadcast theme consisted of attacks on Habayit Hayehudi. Its ads claimed that behind its young millionaire leader Bennett were several radical-right candidates and extreme rabbis. Labour promised economic and social hand-outs, while taking money from the rich. It also claimed that the middle class would pay lower taxes. Its main slogan was: 'It can be better here.' Most parties in many other countries could have used this same bland motto. Shas broadcast its spiritual guide, the nonagenarian former Chief Rabbi Ovadia Yosef, calling people to vote for it. It presented itself as the natural choice for those in lower income brackets.

The division of airtime

Broadcast airtime is divided according to the number of seats in the outgoing Knesset. Parties not represented were only given a few minutes. This meant for instance that Yesh Atid, which according to polls would receive around 10 seats, hardly appeared on television and radio at all.

It also implied that Likud/Yisrael Beiteinu had several ads in each election broadcast. Kadima was next in line for broadcasting time. Polls continued to show that it was doubtful whether the party would pass the election threshold. Kadima appealed in its advertisements to voters by stating that Mofaz had been a good Minister of Defence and Chief of Staff. His political performance as party leader had been poor however.

In the meantime, the Palestinians continued to undermine the claims of those parties which asserted that peace is possible. Palestinian Authority Chairman Mahmoud Abbas and head of Hamas's political bureau Khaled Mashaal met in Cairo to discuss reconciliation between their two organizations. Netanyahu said this showed that Abbas did not want peace, as he gave 'a hug to the head of the terrorist organization who announced only a month ago that Israel should be wiped off the map'. Netanyahu added: 'A leader who desires peace does not behave this way.'[97]

Far more important to the Israeli public was the impact of the severe weather conditions. Torrential rain fell for several days and interrupted normal life in many places. It was followed by snow in Jerusalem and other high-lying areas.

The last days of the campaign

The last days of the election campaign hardly enlivened the Israeli public more than the weeks before. Yet there were two disparate, important news items. It was announced that Israel's budget deficit in 2012 reached 39 billion shekels or 4.2% of gross domestic product, much higher than had been forecast, despite the growth in GDP of 3.3%.[98] This news could have given the centre-left opposition parties an opportunity to stress that the Netanyahu government was practising election economics and that its much-touted economic success of the past few years included major flaws.

However, several opposition leaders went for overkill. Livni said: 'The political irresponsibility and flawed priorities' of the Netanyahu government would 'lead Israel to bankruptcy'.[99] She sounded as if Israel was on the verge of becoming a second Greece. Her claim that Israel should change its priorities away from the settlements was heard less however.

Yachimovich used somewhat similar language, stating: 'The data about the huge deficit demonstrates the social hell and economic chaos we are facing here if Netanyahu is re-elected Prime Minister, Heaven forbid.'[100] Labour was hardly in a position to criticize the government, however, as it proposed to spend more rather than less.

On another note, former Prime Minister Ehud Olmert, who supported Kadima, accused Netanyahu of having wasted 11 billion shekels in the past two years on what he termed 'military delusions'. He referred to projects related to the Iranian nuclear threat.[101] Netanyahu called Olmert's claims 'bizarre' and 'irresponsible'.[102]

In European Union countries, the rule is that budget deficits should not exceed 3% of GDP. Yet in 2011, the budget deficit of the 17 countries of the eurozone amounted to 4.1%, reduced from 6.2% in 2010.[103] Israel is thus far from an economic precipice. It was clear to all that the new Knesset would have to decide on important budget cuts, yet this did not become a major campaign issue, because there was little mileage in it for most parties.

Obama's concern

A second item received more public attention. On 15 January, American commentator Jeffrey Goldberg wrote on the Bloomberg website that President Barack Obama had channelled public messages to Israel through him on the Palestinian and Iranian issues on several occasions in the past four years. He claimed that in private conversations, Obama had expressed concern that Netanyahu was leading Israel to 'international isolation'. Goldberg suggested that the US might change its diplomatic position toward Israel which would isolate it more at the UN or when confronted with European initiatives.[104]

The Likud spokesmen initially reacted by saying that Netanyahu would continue to resist international pressure as he had done in the past few years.[105] A few days later, Netanyahu admitted that Obama and he had differences, 'especially on the best way to achieve and advance a defensible peace with the Palestinians'. He mentioned that there had often been divergences of view with the American administration since the establishment of Israel in 1948. He gave as examples those between Ben Gurion and US Secretary of State George Marshall and those between Ariel Sharon and George W. Bush.[106]

Livni, who tried to cash in on Obama's criticism, saw her support in the polls continue to fall. Polls put now Hatnuah far behind Labour and well below Yesh Atid.[107] The impact of Goldberg's revelations was possibly minor because Obama is not popular among Israeli Jews. Before the American elections, a poll in Israel asked which presidential candidate would be preferable concerning Israel's interests. Fifty-seven per cent of Israeli Jews preferred Romney, while 22% said Obama. Among Israeli Arabs, Obama was the preferred candidate.[108] In another development, Lieberman said that he would resign from political life if he were convicted on the fraud and breach of trust charges against him.[109]

With election day close, various parties continued to stake out claims for entering a probable Netanyahu-appointed government. Yesh Atid repeated that it would only join the government if army and national service were introduced for all young adults equally.[110] Bennett on the right as well as Livni and Lapid on the left called for a unity government, albeit with different partners.[111]

According to campaign rules, published polls were no longer permitted after Friday 18 January. This brought their flood to an end. Final polls continued to show that parties of the centre-right together with ultra-Orthodox parties would enjoy a majority in the 19th Knesset.[112] In its last advertisements, Likud/Yisrael Beiteinu partly switched direction somewhat, emphasizing Netanyahu being a family man.

Election night

What months of campaigning lacked in excitement was partly compensated for on election night. The results initially showed a dead heat between the centre-right/ ultra-Orthodox and the centre-left together with the Arab parties. The votes of the soldiers were counted a few days later and moved the results to 61/59 as Habayit Hayehudi received a twelfth seat at the expense of the Arab Raam Taal party.

Likud/Yisrael Beiteinu results were at the lowest point of all polls in the campaign, receiving 31 seats. The election's great surprise was Yesh Atid's 19 seats, far beyond what any recent poll had indicated. Labour came in third place with 15 seats.

The ultra-Orthodox parties, Shas and United Torah Judaism maintained, or increased their strength with 11 and seven seats respectively. Arab parties remained stable with 11 seats. Meretz doubled its representation from three to six MKs, while Kadima received two seats. Table 1 below contains the official results of the elections:

Table 1.   Final official results of the elections for the 19th Knesset.

List of candidates	Percentage of valid votes	Number of mandates (Knesset seats)
Likud-Israel Beiteinu	23.34	31
Yesh Atid	14.33	19
Israel Labour Party (Avoda)	11.39	15
Habayit Hayehudi	9.12	12
Shas	8.75	11
United Torah Judaism	5.16	7
Hatnuah	4.99	6
Meretz	4.55	6
United Arab List (Raam Taal)	3.65	4
Hadash	2.99	4
National Democratic Assembly	2.56	3
Kadima	2.08	2

Source: "Final official results of the Elections for the Nineteenth Knesset," Central Elections Committee's website, http://www.bechirot.gov.il/elections19/eng/list/results_eng.aspx (accessed January 1, 2014).

One probable conclusion to be drawn from the results is that the Israeli public prefers new faces and yet unproven politicians. This may be mainly due to a malaise with existing parties, their leaders and parliamentarians. Further indication of this was the success of another newcomer, Habayit Hayehudi's Bennett.

There were probably more polls published this time around than during any previous elections. Yet their limitations were also never exposed as much. The large number of undecided voters – some even choosing which party to vote for in the polling booth itself – greatly reduced the polls' value. With all of the confusion and uncertainty, few people would be surprised if Israel's next parliamentary elections were to take place well before 2017 as scheduled.

Disclosure statement
No potential conflict of interest was reported by the author.

Notes on contributor
Manfred Gerstenfeld is the Emeritus Chairman of the Jerusalem Center for Public Affairs, Israel.

Notes

1. Jonathan Lis, "Israel's Knesset Votes to Disband, Hold Early Elections on January 22," *Haaretz*, October 15, 2012.
2. Gil Hoffman, "Post Poll: 'Center-Left Mega-Party' Would Beat PM," *Jerusalem Post*, October 11, 2012.
3. "Israeli PM Olmert Hands in Resignation," *CNN World*, September 21, 2008.
4. Isabel Kershner, "Former Israeli Premier Gets Suspended Sentence," *New York Times,* September 24, 2012.
5. Nir Hasson, "State Appeals Olmert's Graft Acquittals, Sentence in Conviction," *Haaretz*, November 7, 2012.
6. Anshel Pfeffer, "Tzipi Livni to Challenge Bibi in her Return to Politics," *Jewish Chronicle*, October 25, 2012.
7. JPost.com Staff, "Poll: Yacimovich Preferred Leader of Center-Left," *Jerusalem Post*, November 1, 2012.
8. "Kadima Quits Israel Government over Conscription Law," *BBC News*, July 17, 2012.
9. Lahav Harkov, "Right Loses 4 Seats from Likud Beytenu Merger," *Jerusalem Post*, November 2, 2012.
10. Jonathan Lis, "Netanyahu Supporters Scramble to Dissuade Kahlon from Running on Separate Ticket," *Haaretz*, November 2, 2012.
11. Yair Ettinger, "Yishai Heads Shas Party List, Deri Takes Second Place," *Haaretz*, December 6, 2012.
12. Jonathan Lis and Eli Ashkenazi, "Kibbutz leader withdraws from Labor primary," *Haaretz*, November 1, 2012.
13. Harkov, "Right Loses 4 Seats from Likud Beytenu Merger."
14. "New Poll Predicts Kadima Won't Make 2% Voting Threshold in January Elections," *Times of Israel*, November 3, 2012.
15. Roi Mandel, "Meretz Locks Knesset List, Eyes Election," *Ynetnews*, November 12, 2012.
16. Lahav Harkov, "Slomiansky, Shaked Top Habayit Hayehudi List," *Jerusalem Post*, November 15, 2012.
17. "MK Uri Ariel Elected to Head National Union," *Israel National News*, November 18, 2012.
18. Chaim Levinson, "Far-right MKs Unite to Form New Party," *Haaretz*, November 13, 2012.
19. Yossi Verter, "Tzipi Livni Pushing Shimon Peres to Run for Israel's Premiership," *Haaretz*, November 8, 2012.

20. Gil Hoffman, "Polls: Huge Support for Operation, Not Invasion," *Jerusalem Post*, November 19, 2012.
21. "Mofaz: Gaza Op Long Overdue, Must Continue," *Ynetnews*, November 18, 2012.
22. Times of Israel Staff, "Ashkelon Fireman, 2 Residents Suffer Shrapnel Injuries from Gaza Rockets," *Times of Israel*, November 18, 2012, 17–18.
23. Hassan Shaalan, "Arab MKs Observe Moment of Silence for Gaza 'Martyrs'," *Ynetnews*, November 17, 2012.
24. "Poll: Israelis Dissatisfied with Cease-fire," *Guardian*, November 23, 2012.
25. Gil Ronen, "Poll: Ceasefire Weakens Likud, Strengthens Bennett & Ben-Ari," *Israel National News*, November 22, 2012.
26. Gil Hoffman, "Livni to Split Center-Left with New Centrist Party," *Jerusalem Post*, November 22, 2012.
27. Yoel Goldman, "Yachimovich Urges Livni to Join Labor," *Times of Israel*, November 24, 2012.
28. Avi Cohen and Shlomo Cesana "Livni's Suitors Come Calling," *Israel Hayom*, November 26, 2012.
29. Gil Ronen, "MK Danon in Push to Disqualify Zoabi," *Israel National News*, November 24, 2012.
30. Yuval Karni, Moran Azulay, "Likud Primaries: Feiglin In, Begin and Meridor Out," *Ynetnews*, November 27, 2012.
31. Ibid.
32. Ronen, "Poll: Ceasefire Weakens Likud, Strengthens Bennett & Ben-Ari."
33. Gil Hoffman, "Barak Pushing Meridor to Head Independence Party," *Jerusalem Post*, December 4, 2012.
34. Roi Mandel, "Independence Party Drops Out of Knesset Race," *Ynetnews*, December 6, 2012.
35. JPost Staff and Gil Hoffman, "Tzipi Livni Launches New Political Party: The Movement," *Jerusalem Post*, November 27, 2012.
36. Times of Israel Staff, "Full Results of Labor Party Primaries," *Times of Israel*, November 30, 2012.
37. Barak Ravid and Jonathan Lis, "Lieberman Unveils his List for Likud Beiteinu Ticket," *Haaretz*, December 4, 2012.
38. Shahar Chai, "Lapid Introduces Yesh Atid's Knesset List," *Ynetnews*, December 2, 2012.
39. Ilan Lior and Jonathan Lis, "Former Labor Party Leader Amram Mitzna Joins Livni's Party," *Haaretz*, December 2, 2012.
40. "Political Parties Present Final Lists for 19th Israeli Knesset," *Haaretz*, December 7, 2012.
41. Ilan Lior, Jonathan Lis, and Haaretz, "Former Labor Chief MK Peretz Joins Livni's Hatnuah Party," *Haaretz*, December 6, 2012.
42. Ibid.
43. Yossi Verter, "Haaretz Poll: Majority of Israelis Say Netanyahu Will Retain Premiership," *Haaretz*, December 10, 2012.
44. Barak Ravid and Jonathan Lis, "Foreign Minister Avigdor Lieberman to Resign Over Indictment Decision," *Haaretz*, December 14, 2012.
45. Jonathan Lis, "Habayit Hayehudi Chairman Retracts Comments on Refusal to Evacuate Settlements," *Haaretz*, December 20, 2012.
46. Telem Yahav, "Elections Committee Bans Zoabi," Ynetnews.com, December 19, 2012.
47. JPost.com Staff, "High Court allows Balad MK Zoabi to run for Knesset," *Jerusalem Post*, December 30, 2012.
48. "Morsi mouths 'Amen' as Egyptian preacher urges "Allah, destroy the Jews'," *The Times of Israel*, October 21, 2012.

49. Elad Benari, "Morsi in 2010: No Negotiations with 'Descendants of Apes'," *Israel National News*, January 4, 2013.
50. JPost.com Staff and Reuters, "Mashaal: First Gaza, then Ramallah, then Jerusalem," *Jerusalem Post*, December 8, 2012.
51. Daniel Siryoti and Israel Hayom Staff, "Palestinians Prefer Hamas Leader Haniyeh Over Abbas, Poll Shows," *Israel Hayom*, December 18, 2012.
52. Elad Benari, "European Members of Security Council Condemn Israel," *Israel National News*, December 19, 2012.
53. Gil Hoffman, "Poll Finds Lieberman Indictment had Negligible Impact," *Jerusalem Post*, December 20, 2012.
54. Gil Hoffman, "Yair Shamir Attacks Bayit Yehudi Anglo Campaign," *Jerusalem Post*, December 19, 2012.
55. Gil Hoffman, Ben Hartman, and Jeremy Sharon, "Likud Declares War on Rivals in Center-Right Bloc," *Jerusalem Post*, December 24, 2012.
56. JPost.com Staff, "PM: 'Refusal' Advocates won't Sit in my Government," *Jerusalem Post*, December 21, 2012.
57. Lahav Harkov, "Committee Fines Likud Beytenu for Anonymous Anti-Bennett Ads," *Jerusalem Post*, December 27, 2012.
58. Gil Hoffman, "Feiglin: Bashing of Bayit Yehudi's Bennet will Cost Likud Votes," *Jerusalem Post*, December 24, 2012.
59. Gil Hoffman, "Bayit Yehudi Gains 3 Seats in a Week, 'Post' Poll Finds," *Jerusalem Post*, December 28, 2012.
60. Gil Hoffman, "Bennett: Netanyahu Must Take Back his Statement of Support for Palestinian State," *Jerusalem Post*, December 25, 2012.
61. "Views of the Israeli Public on Israeli Security and Resolution of the Arab–Israeli Conflict – 19 December 2012," *Jerusalem Center for Public Affairs*, December 19, 2012.
62. Yonah Jeremy Bob and Herb Keinon, "Weinstein Submits Updated Liberman Indictment to Knesset," *Jerusalem Post*, December 28, 2012.
63. Lahav Harkov, "Lieberman to Chair Defense C'tee Amid Legal Woes," *Jerusalem Post*, December 25, 2012.
64. Elad Benari, "Bennett: Netanyahu Planning Leftist Coalition," *Israel National News*, December 25, 2012.
65. Jeremy Sharon, "Shas Will be in Next Gov't, Will Protect the Poor," *Jerusalem Post*, December 26, 2012.
66. Gil Hoffman and Lahav Harkov, "Livni Reportedly in Contact with PM's Aides about Reclaiming Foreign Ministry," *Jerusalem Post*, December 26, 2012.
67. David Lev, "PM: Livni Will Not be a Part of Next Government", *Israel National News*, December 27, 2012.
68. "Yachimovich Challenges Netanyahu to Public Debate," *Ynet News*, December 24, 2012.
69. Adiv Sterman, "Labor Leader Calls for Immediate Renewal of Israeli–Palestinian Peace Talks," *Times of Israel*, December 23, 2012.
70. Shiri Hadar, "A New Red Line: Lapid's 'Homage' to Bibi," *Ynet News*, December 25, 2012.
71. Adrian Filut, "Fischer Contradicts Steinitz on Tax Hikes," *Globes*, December 27, 2012.
72. Gil Hoffman, "'Post' Poll: Likud Beytenu Hits New Low of 32 Mandates," *Jerusalem Post*, January 4, 2013.
73. Ilan Ben Zion, "Amid Uproar, Netanyahu Reportedly Reaffirms Commitment to Two-State Solution," *Times of Israel*, December 31, 2012.

74. Maayana Miskin, "Lieberman: I Support a Palestinian State," *Israel National News*, January 6, 2013.
75. Tovah Lazaroff, "Likud Politicians Call on Israel to annex Area C," *Jerusalem Post*, January 1, 2013.
76. Gil Hoffman, Tamara Zieve, "Ya'alon Speaks against Founding of a Palestinian State," *Jerusalem Post*, January 12, 2013.
77. Elad Benari, "Netanyahu is a 'Zigazagger,' Says Shamir," *Israel National News*, January 4, 2013.
78. Lahav Harkov, "Shamir Retracts Remarks about PM's 'Zigzags'," *Jerusalem Post*, January 5, 2013.
79. Richard Spencer, "Israel Will Cease to Exist within a Decade, says Muslim Brotherhood Official," *Telegraph*, January 1, 2013.
80. Khaled Abu Toameh "PA Scoffs at Hamas Offer to Take Over West Bank," *Jerusalem Post*, January 1, 2013.
81. Lahav Harkov, Herb Keinon, and Greer Fay Cashman, "Peres Unleashes Political Maelstrom with Pro-Abbas Remarks to Envoys," *Jerusalem Post*, December 31, 2012.
82. Melanie Lidman and Gil Hoffman, "Police Weighing Possible Indictment Against Feiglin," *Jerusalem Post*, January 2, 2013.
83. Stuart Winer and Gabe Fisher, "Likud Hardliner Suggests Paying Palestinian Families to Emigrate from West Bank," *Times of Israel*, January 2, 2013.
84. Israel Hayom Staff and Associated Press, "Likud's Hard Right Criticizes Netanyahu for Attacks on Bennett," *Israel Hayom*, December 25, 2012.
85. Gil Ronen, "Yesha Leaders: Likud, Stop Attacking Bayit Yehudi," *Israel National News*, January 3, 2013.
86. Asher Zeiger, "Shas Will Support Territorial Concessions in Future Peace Deal, Asserts One of Party's Leaders," *Times of Israel*, January 3, 2013.
87. Hagai Golan, "Deri: Shas Won't Relinquish Housing Portfolio," *Globes*, December 27, 2012.
88. Gil Ronen, "Deri Apologizes, Then Does It Again," *Israel National News*, December 31, 2012.
89. Lahav Harkov, "Yacimovich: Labor Won't Join Netanyahu Coalition," *Jerusalem Post*, January 4, 2013.
90. Ibid
91. Niv Elis, Nadav Shemer, and Lahav Harkov, "Under Labor, Israeli Economy would be Worse than Spain's," *Jerusalem Post*, December 31, 2012.
92. "Livni Reportedly to Quit Politics – Again – Should Knesset Bid Prove Disappointing," *Times of Israel*, December 30, 2012.
93. Gilad Morag, "Lapid: Yachimovich Leading us to Messianic Government," *Ynet News*, January 3, 2013.
94. Shlomo Cesana, Mati Tuchfeld, and Avi Cohen, "Knives Come Out in Center-Left after Unity Meet Goes Sour," *Israel HaYom*, January 8, 2013.
95. Yaron Druckman, "State Comptroller Finds Misconduct in Harpaz Affair," *Ynetnews*, January 6, 2013.
96. Stephan Miller, "Latest Polls Confirm High Level of Undecided Voters, Indicate Fall in Support for Tzipi Livni," *Times of Israel*, January 11, 2013.
97. Elad Benari, "Netanyahu Criticizes Abbas, Livni Criticizes Netanyahu," *Israel National News*, January 11, 2013.
98. Steven Scheer, "Israel Budget Deficit Dents Netanyahu's 'Mr Economy' Image," *UK Reuters*, January 14, 2013.
99. "Treasury Posts Budget Deficit of NIS 39B," *Ynet News*, January 13, 2013.
100. Ibid

101. Jonathan Lis and Gilli Cohen, "Olmert: Netanyahu Spent NIS 11 Billion on Adventurous Fantasies," *Haaretz*, January 12, 2013.
102. Asher Zeiger, "Defense Sources Back Up Olmert in Iran Spending Spat," *Times of Israel*, January 14, 2013.
103. David Jolly, "European Countries Slashed Deficits in 2011, Data Show," *New York Times*, October 22, 2012.
104. Barak Ravid, "Netanyahu Associates Brush Off Obama Criticism: PM Won't Give In to International Pressure," *Haaretz*, January 15, 2013.
105. Ibid.
106. Herb Keinon and Steve Linde, "Netanyahu to 'Post': I Won't Uproot Masses of Jews," *Jerusalem Post*, January 18, 2013.
107. Gil Hoffman, "'Post' Poll: Likud Beytenu Holds Steady at 34 Seats," *Jerusalem Post*, January 18, 2013.
108. Herb Keinon, "Poll: Israeli Jews Favor Romney by Wide Margin," *Jerusalem Post*, October 28, 2012.
109. Asher Zeiger and Times of Israel Staff, "Liberman Says he'll Leave Politics if Convicted," *Times of Israel*, January 14, 2013.
110. Jeremy Sharon, "Yesh Atid: Universal Service Plan 'Red Line' for Joining Government," *Jerusalem Post*, January 16, 2013.
111. "Lapid, Livni, Bennett Call for National Unity Government," *Jerusalem Post*, January 17, 2013.
112. "Hawkish Bloc Leads in polls Ahead of Israel Vote," *Associated Press*, January 18, 2013.

The Peculiar Victory of The National Camp in the 2013 Israeli Election

Arie Perliger[a] and Eran Zaidise[b]

[a]Department of Social Sciences, United States Military Academy, West Point, NY, USA;
[b]Department of Political Science, Western Galilee College, Akko, Israel

This article argues that attempts to characterize the outcome of the elections to the 19th Knesset as a defeat of the Israeli right are misleading. By using a three-dimensional analysis of the ideological makeup of the Knesset, based on the ideological manifestos of the parties, the socio-demographic profiles of Knesset members and analyses of election results utilizing electoral data and socio-demographic data obtained from Israel's Central Bureau of Statistics (CBS), the article claims that the 19th Knesset is no less right-leaning than its predecessor. Hence, contrary to some commentators in both the media and academia, the 2013 elections represent a true landmark for the settlers. For the first time since the movement appeared in the 1970s, it managed to obtain a solid base in the Knesset.

That which hath been is that which shall be, and that which hath been done is that which shall be done; and there is nothing new under the sun. (Ecclesiastes: 1, 9)

It was disorienting to observe the coverage of the elections for the 19th Knesset through the eyes of the international media. Prior to the elections, media outlets all over the world were reporting about the 'radical right-wing tide' and displayed concern that the new cabinet would be extremely hawkish. Once the first exit polls were aired, pre-eminent pundits like Aaron David Miller released a sigh of relief.[1] The new consensus was that Israel had 'changed its course'. As Israelis who monitored the elections very closely, we were puzzled. The media in the United States and Europe had little interest in domestic political issues such as the enlistment of ultra-Orthodox youths to the IDF, or the economic difficulties of the middle class. They were preoccupied with one issue: the potential effect of the elections on the Israeli–Palestinian conflict. The flood of commentaries regarding the 'unique opportunity for a renewal of the peace process' made us feel like we were following a different story altogether. In this article, we aim to bridge the perceptual gap between the new government's image in the international press and the traits and makeup of its members and voters.

This article argues that any attempt to characterize the outcome of the elections to the 19th Knesset as a defeat of the Israeli right is misleading. By using a three-dimensional analysis of the ideological makeup of the Knesset, based on the ideological manifestos of the parties, the socio-demographic profiles of Knesset members and analyses of election results utilizing electoral data and socio-demographic data obtained from Israel's Central Bureau of Statistics (CBS), we claim that the 19th Knesset is expected to prove no less right-leaning than its predecessor. Hence, contrary to some commentators in both the media and academia, we contend that the 2013 elections represent a true landmark for the settlers. For the first time since the movement appeared in the 1970s, it managed to obtain a solid base in the Knesset. This unprecedented electoral success will serve as the icing on the cake for an already successful endeavour. Moreover, we will illustrate that the gap between the Israeli right and far right is progressively diminishing and that the latter was able in the last few years to mobilize new supporters, mainly from the socio-economic centre of the Israeli electorate.

Ideological mapping of the Israeli right

Before one can assess the achievements of the Israeli right in the 2013 elections, one must first delineate the boundaries of this political camp. Two unique traits turn Israel into a challenging case for comparative analysis of political parties and elections. First, Israel is a small country (8019 square miles) and its approximately 8 million citizens are deeply divided along national, religious, ethnic, economic and ideological lines. The nationwide proportional representation electoral system with its relatively low representation threshold (2%) generates a highly fragmented parliament. Thirty-three political parties participated in the 2013 elections. Out of these, 12 managed to surpass the 2% threshold and gain representation in the 19th Knesset. Second, since the late 1960s, the main criterion which was used to determine if a party leans to the right or to the left was its location on the dovish–hawkish scale.[2] The use of such a one-dimensional criterion left many parties, most notably the ultra-Orthodox ones, without a clear designation. In order to overcome this recurrent predicament, we suggest a more nuanced approach.

As mentioned in a recent study on the American far right:

> the study of far-right parties has for years suffered from terminological chaos … it is not merely that different scholars have used different terms to describe these parties, but that there are also disagreements regarding the kind of ideological foundations that constitute the far-right paradigm.[3]

In order to overcome this conceptual inconsistency and to identify the political parties that are part of the Israeli far-right spectrum, we used six major ideological elements that commonly reappear and are highly consensual in the literature regarding their association with the far-right ideological framework. Israeli parties with an ideological platform or rhetoric – during the last elections – which emphasized at least two of these ideological elements were considered in our analysis as right-wing parties. This will allow us not just to identify which Israeli parties are promoting a far-right ideology, but also identify distinctions between the different actors comprising the Israeli far-right spectrum; in other words, to answer the question: which Israeli far-right parties are more extreme than others?

The first four elements – internal homogeneity, nativism, exclusionism and xenophobia – are related to various mechanisms defining the boundaries of the collective or a defined group (i.e. between insiders and outsiders). While internal homogeneity reflects the aspiration that all residents of a polity will share the same national origin and ethnic characteristics,[4] nativism represents a wider implementation of this concept by not merely rejecting the incorporation and recognition of those embodying different ethnic and national traits as part of the nation, but also rejecting and distancing oneself from what appear to be foreign norms and practices.[5] The nativism of the Israeli radical right consists of three elements. The first, which is paradoxical by nature, is the aspiration that the individuals who live within the borders of the sovereign state of Israel belong to the 'Jewish ethnicity', even if they were not born in Israel. Native Palestinians with Israeli citizenship, foreign workers and other individuals who do not belong to the Jewish ethnic collective do not qualify as ethnically Jewish and therefore are not entitled to full citizen rights. In a more extreme version of nativism, such individuals are not even allowed to live in the state of Israel. The second component of nativism is the absolute and exclusive right of the Jewish people over greater Israel.[6] In the updated version, this includes the borders of the sovereign state of Israel as well the territories that were occupied in 1967: the West Bank, the Golan Heights, the Sinai Peninsula, the Gaza Strip and the jewel in the crown, East Jerusalem. The third component is the rejection of those liberal or multicultural ideas that pose a challenge to the two first components.

Xenophobia involves behaviours and sentiments derived from hate and hostility toward groups that are perceived as alien or distinct and exclusionism is the practical manifestation of these sentiments on the communal or state level. Practically, outsiders are excluded from specific spheres of the social, economic and political arena, such as the labour market, the educational system, residential areas and social gatherings of various sorts.[7]

The remaining two ideological elements completing our six far-right traits are affinity toward traditional values and anti-democratic sentiments which reflect the aspiration of far-right groups to shape the political culture. More specifically, affinity toward traditional values represents an aspiration to restore or preserve values and practices that are part of the heritage of the nation.[8] Anti-democratic dispositions are mostly a reflection of the difficulty of far-right parties to reconcile tensions between core nationalist elements such as internal homogenization and nativism and the liberal-democratic value system which emphasizes civil rights, minority rights and the balance of power.[9]

This conceptualization of far-right ideology allows us to proceed and more accurately measure the actual strength of this ideological stream, comparing the current Knesset makeup to previous ones. Moreover, it will reveal that the gap between the Israeli right and far right is progressively diminishing, as today it includes just a small part of the Likud party. Hence our decision to focus mainly, but not exclusively on the Israeli far right.

A downfall of the national camp? The true ideological composition of the 19th Knesset

As noted above, the relative success of parties such as Yesh Atid (literally meaning 'There is a future'), Hatnuah, and even Meretz, facilitated a perception that indeed the tipping point of the Israeli legislator is transitioning from its former right-of-centre position to the centre-left of the Israeli ideological spectrum and has the potential to become more supportive of future conciliation processes between Israelis and Palestinians. However, a more in-depth look into the results and the practice of a comparative perspective that takes into consideration changes in the composition of the Knesset over time reveals a different picture, if not an entirely opposed one.

To begin with, and as can be observed in Table 1, the parties which hold far-right ideological sentiments – shaded in grey – actually increased their total number of seats in comparison to the two previous Knesset election. They now hold more than a third of the overall seats in the Israeli parliament (41 out of the overall 120 seats). This number represents a new record for the Israeli far right, which showed consistent growth in the last three decades. Thus, after breaking the 20-seat barrier in the 12th Knesset with 25 seats, and the 30-seat barrier in the 15th Knesset with 35 seats, the Israeli far right's growth seems one of the few consistent features in a relatively chaotic Israeli party system. In terms of ideological emphasis, it seems that sentiments of nativism and support for internal homogeneity are the most visible within the Israeli far-right discourse.

The table also shows that the rise of the Israeli far right is less a result of electoral growth within the ultra-Orthodox parties (Shas and Yehadut Hatora) – which it seems already maximized their electoral potential in the early 2000s – but more a consequence of the growing number of secular Israelis departing from traditional and established parties and supporting various secular, ultra-nationalistic platforms. Even the National-Religious party (now called Habayit Hayehudi, meaning 'The Jewish Home') identified this trend and the mobilization potential of this new electorate of secular-nationalist Israelis. This party thus emphasized a nationalistic and civilian agenda in its recent campaign, rather than its religious facets which dominated its previous public messages. It is not a coincidence, then, that for the first time a secular woman was placed – via the party's primaries – near the top of the party's candidate list. Ayelet Shaked was elected to the fifth place on the party's list. Furthermore, during the post-election negotiations, the party was determined not to join any coalition which includes ultra-Orthodox parties. This together with the call for equal military service for the ultra-Orthodox community helps set a public agenda intended as

Table 1. Parties with far-right tendencies in the last three Knesset

Party/ideological component (number of seats)	Internal homogeneity	Nativism	Exclusionism	Xenophobia	Traditional values	Anti-democratic
17th Knesset (38 seats)						
Shas (12)	√	√		√	√	√
Yisrael Beiteinu (11)	√	√	√	√		
National Union (9)		√			√	√
Yahadut Hatora (6)	√	√				
Kadima (29)						
Labour-Meimad (19)						
Likud (12)						
Gil (7)						
Meretz (5)						
Ta'al (4)						
Hadash (3)						
Balad (3)						
18th Knesset (38 seats)						
Yisrael Beiteinu (15)	√	√		√	√	√
Shas (11)	√	√	√	√	√	√
Yahadut Hatora (5)		√			√	
National Union (4)	√	√			√	
Habayit Hayehudi (3)		√			√	
Kadima (28)						
Likud (27)						
Labour Party (13)						
Ta'al (4)						
Hadash (4)						
Meretz (3)						
Balad (3)						
19th Knesset (41 seats)						
Yisrael Beiteinu (11)	√	√		√		

(Continued)

Table 1 – (*continued*)

Party/ideological component (number of seats)	Internal homogeneity	Nativism	Exclusionism	Xenophobia	Traditional values	Anti-democratic
Habayit Hayehudi (12)		√				
Shas (11)	√	√	√		√	√
Yahadut Hatora (7)		√		√	√	√
Likud (20)						
Yesh Atid (19)						
Labour Party (15)						
Hatnuah (6)						
Meretz (6)						
Ta'al (4)						
Hadash (4)						
Balad (3)						
Kadima (2)						

much for a non-religious crowd as for its traditional, mostly religious, settler base which have in the last elections made up most of this party's electorate.

The centre-left parties in many ways followed campaign tactics set forth by the HaBayit HaYehudi, marginalizing issues which in the past were the pillars of their ideological platform – i.e. the future of the occupied territories and the Israeli–Arab conflict. For example, Yesh Atid, a new party established less than two years before the elections by media personality Yair Lapid and aiming to mobilize the electorate from the centre of the political spectrum, focused on civilian issues such as the economic struggles of the middle class and the need to ensure that ultra-Orthodox youths will also share the security burden and serve in the IDF. Further to the left, the Labour party adopted the same rhetorical strategy by avoiding emphasis on its long-term opposition to the settlement project and its ongoing support for the 'two-state solution'. Led by Shelly Yachimovich, also a former journalist, the Labour party campaign built upon her successful legislative achievements in the realm of welfare economics and working class rights. Labour based most of its propaganda efforts in convincing Israelis that it could provide effective solutions to the deteriorating quality of life in Israel and the collapsing welfare services. Yachimovich even emphasized Labour's opposition to attempts to de-legitimize the settler community, as well as to link the major Israeli investments in the West Bank to the difficulties of the Israeli economy.[10]

The result of the above-mentioned dynamics were twofold. Both strengthened the Israeli far-right agenda. First, the Israeli–Palestinian conflict became marginalized into almost a non-issue in the last elections. This indirectly further affirmed the Israeli far-right's long-term assertion that the 'two-state solution' is neither viable nor legitimate and that Israel has no partner among the Palestinians at the negotiation table. Second, it further reinforced the process of marginalization and de-legitimization of a left-wing ideological alternative. Lapid, for example, emphasized his refusal of any territorial concessions in Jerusalem. He constantly refused attempts to establish a political alliance with centre-left political parties – i.e. Labour and Tzipi Livni's party, 'Hatnuah'. Even Yachimovich adopted a rhetoric that emphasized the responsibility of the Palestinian side to the lack of progress in the peace process, thus strengthening the common right-wing narrative that peace with the Palestinians is unattainable, even if desired by Israel.

In summing up the above, we claim that the right-wing electoral success is not only on the rise in terms of the number of members of the Knesset (MKs) representing right-wing parties, but is also beginning to penetrate the mobilization campaigns of centre and left-wing parties. The Israeli far right has been able to impose its rhetorical paradigm on the election's discourse while marginalizing attempts to provide a coherent alternative ideological framework. But can the growing prominence of the Israeli far-right ideological paradigm be explained solely as a result of its ability to shape the public discourse, or are right-wing politicians and parties also gaining more prominence throughout the political system and mainly the legislative branch? The next section will try to provide an answer to this question.

Settling in the Knesset? Or settling in the cabinet?

In the weeks before and following the 2013 elections, the Israeli media, as well as some academics, emphasized the growing number and influence within the Knesset of representatives from communities which since the early 1980s became the most significant electorate of the Israeli right-wing parties. These mainly include the settler community, ultra-Orthodox and religious-Zionists. Here again, in-depth examination reveals that the picture is more multi-faceted.

Since the election of the 15th Knesset, the number of MKs residing in the West Bank or the Gaza Strip – in the 15th Knesset there were 10 such MKs – has been disproportional to the percentage of settlers in the entire Israeli population. However, the proportion of MKs living in the West Bank has not increased significantly since then. While the 16th Knesset included 11 MKs who were residing in settlements – whether in the West Bank or the Gaza Strip – the number decreased to 10 again in the 18th Knesset and remained the same following the elections to the 19th Knesset. Following the last elections the overall number of ultra-Orthodox and religious members of the Knesset rose to 39 or 32.5% of the total, a record number. This was a 34% increase compared to the 18th Knesset. This however does not necessarily represent an increase in the power of the far right, as at least 10 of these MKs were elected under the auspices of centre or centre-right parties. Four Orthodox MKs were elected on the Yesh Atid and Hatnua lists and an additional six on that of the Likud.

These figures should, however, be considered in the light of a growing body of literature which claims a marginalization in the importance of the Israeli legislature in shaping public policies.[11] The major argument is that the settler movement was able to develop alternative mechanisms, mainly via the public administration and the security establishment, to promote and protect their interests.[12] The result of the last elections and especially the composition of the new cabinet suggest that this practice reached a new level. The most important ministries, in terms of their ability to support the infrastructure of the settlement project, are under the direct control of representatives of the settler community and their close ideological allies. The Housing Ministry is now headed by Uri Ariel, of the Habayit Hayehudi party. For more than a decade (1989–99) he headed the Yesha Council, the formal leadership body of the settler community and later the division for settlements at the Ministry of Defence. The latter was considered by many as the main mechanism utilized by the Israeli government to support the settlement project. The Ministry of Agriculture and Rural Development is headed by Yair Shamir (Yisrael Beiteinu). He is the son of former Likud leader and Prime Minister Yitzhak Shamir and a strong supporter of the settlement project. Shamir criticized Netanyahu before the election because of his inconsistent position toward the peace process. Furthermore, Naftali Bennett, leader of the Habayit Hayehudi, is Minister of Industry, Commerce and Employment. Uzi Landau (Yisrael Beiteinu) is Minister of Tourism. These two head ministries which have significant developmental resources. Indeed the Tourism Ministry was utilized in the last few years as a major channel for site development in the West Bank.[13] Finally, the head of the Knesset Budget Committee – one of the most powerful Knesset committees – with significant authority to monitor and direct transfer of financial resources is Nissan Slomiansky, a settler and parliamentarian of the Habayit Hayehudi. To conclude, while the settlers did not increase their overall numbers in the legislature, they were able to further enhance their influence at the top levels of the executive branch by effectively controlling ministries which are crucial for the ongoing maintenance and expansion of the settlements. The other components of the coalition hold ministries which, while impacting significantly on strategic policies such as Defence, Treasury and Justice, have limited impact on the actual channelling of resources needed to implement the political agenda of the settlers.

The Israeli voter – 2013

In order to gain a better perspective on the nature of the electorate of the Israeli right, we have used the results of the last elections and looked into their association with some basic socio-demographic traits. Overall, our findings correspond with our assessment regarding the expansion of the electoral base of the Israeli right.

Two primary sources of data were merged into a single database for the purpose of our analyses. The first set of data including electoral results at the voting booth level was obtained from the Central Election Committee following the 2013 elections.[14] The second set of data was obtained from the Central Bureau of Statistics. It contains municipality, city and settlement data concerning chief socio-demographic characteristics. Because neighbourhood-level socio-demographic data could not be obtained to match exact voting booth addresses, these data was matched on a city/municipality/settlement level, grouping together several voting booths if they belong to the same city/town. This, of course, overlooks the existing differences especially within the larger and more diverse cities, but still allows for a good overall picture of the spatial characteristics of Israeli voting behaviour and its relationship to the spatial distribution of wealth and socio-demographic traits.

When observing the electorate of the Israeli right as a whole, the strongest predictors for voting for right-wing parties are income ($\alpha = 0.223**$) and level of education ($\alpha = -0.253***$). Hence, Israelis without Bagrut (the high-school diploma which provides access to most universities and institutions of higher education) and with a low income are more inclined to vote for right-wing parties then those with Bagrut and higher incomes. These findings, which appear at first to shed a very negative light on the entire right-wing spectrum, are misleading. If one excludes the Orthodox parties from the analysis, the picture is almost reversed. When looking into the socio-demographic traits of voters for the Likud, Habayit Hayehudi and Otzma we discover that, on a nationwide basis, the level of education is positively correlated with the tendency to vote for these parties ($\alpha = 0.288***$). The level of unemployment is negatively correlated ($\alpha = 0.386***$; more unemployed tend to vote for these parties) so is family size ($\alpha = -0.297***$; people with smaller families tend not to vote for these parties). These trends are indeed consistent with the expectancy for right-wing support worldwide, as the profile of the voter for these parties fits those people who were hit during the economic recession of the last few years: fairly well-educated people with small to average-size families who suffered income loss or lost their jobs because of the recession. As mentioned earlier, it seems that the ability of the Israeli right to mobilize electoral support was based on an emerging constituency of a nationalistic-patriotic middle class, looking for parties which will combine both strong hawkish sentiments with a focus on improving the quality of living for this class.

The other two party groups were less successful in developing new constituencies; the ultra-Orthodox parties, as previous studies show – especially Shas[15] – garner most of their support from lower economic groups. Support for these parties is negatively correlated with income ($\alpha = -0.363***$), family size (also unclear) ($\alpha = -0.465***$), general economic status ($\alpha = -0.387***$) and education ($\alpha = -0.505***$). Centre-left parties mobilize support mainly from the top economic echelons; voting for these parties is positively correlated with economic status ($\alpha = 0.678***$), small families ($\alpha = 0.533***$), income ($\alpha = 0.682***$) and education ($\alpha = 0.552***$). Thus, while each of these party groups mobilizes support from the margins of the electorate – the lower and the top – it seems that the secular and religious-Zionist right continues to broaden its base in the centre, among the secular-religious middle class.

Discussion and concluding remarks

The election results of the 19th Knesset, held on 22 January 2013, emphasized the complexity of Israel's political system. While election results – and even exit polls – were understood almost immediately as paving the way for Benjamin Netanyahu's third term as Prime Minister, the nature and policies of Netanyahu's third government were still unknown.

While some observers interpret the success of new parties like Yesh-Atid and even Habayit Hayehudi as a 'new era in Israeli politics', we contend that former pivots of power – especially in the right wing of Israel's political spectrum – have not lost their hold on the policy process in Israel and have even become stronger and even more deeply rooted in the polity of the state.

The Israeli right may have experienced a setback in terms of 'pure' parliamentary representation and maybe even more so in terms of open visibility in the government's makeup, yet its deep roots have not been cut. We believe that they are still continuing to grow. Electoral success has never been a correct estimate for the political influence of Israel's right-wing extra-parliamentary movements. Until the 2013 elections, the success of the settlers was reversely correlated with their electoral achievements. Since the formation of Gush Emunim, the settlers have never managed to overcome partisan differences and establish a solid parliamentary front. Shortly after Prime Minister Menachem Begin, the champion of the Israeli right, signed the peace treaty with Egypt and instructed his Minister of Defence Ariel Sharon to remove the Israeli settlements in the Sinai Peninsula, several settler leaders have come to the conclusion that they cannot put their fate in the hands of the volatile Israeli public and especially not in those of elected officials. Politically savvy and highly creative, they have dedicated their lives to setting facts on the ground through sophisticated operations behind the scenes. They have studied every law and regulation, raised funds all over the world, identified the bureaucrats who make decisions regarding zoning and land use, recruited them and gradually succeeded in placing their own people in these offices, thus hijacking the bureaucracy and turning it into their own executive wing.

In 2009, they reached a significant milestone when the number of Israeli citizens who reside in the West Bank reached 300,000. According to the Central Bureau of Statistics, there were 342,414 Jewish settlers living in the West Bank in 2011. This is far from marginal. The few remaining optimists among Israeli advocates of the two-state solution rely on the precedents of Israeli withdrawals from Sinai and Gaza. They argue that once an Israeli cabinet reaches a decision to remove settlements, it is entirely capable of implementing it. They have a point. Indeed, in both cases the evacuations were completed despite domestic political strife. However, these analysts rarely mention the numbers. Even the most generous estimates put the number of Israeli settlers in Sinai at 5000 and in Gaza at less than 9000. It is hard to imagine that Israel will have the social, political and economic resilience to relocate more than 300,000 of its citizens especially at this point, when a large part of the state's bureaucracy is fully occupied by the settlers.

Both Israeli and Palestinian negotiators are well aware of the magnitude of the issue and over the years have generated creative and interesting ideas for territorial exchanges. The logic behind these plans is simple. Since most settlements were built in close proximity to the Israeli heartland, the annexation of these heavily populated areas by Israel in exchange for transferring uninhabited Israeli territories to the Palestinians should not compromise the territorial integrity of either state. Under such plans, the number of settlers that will have to relocate comes down to approximately 80,000. They, however, are the most fervent members of the network, the foot soldiers who were happy to carry out the plan of their leaders and settled in the heart of the West Bank in order to subvert any prospect for Palestinian territorial continuity. While these activists may resort to violence, it is the least effective tool in the settlers' arsenal. They are highly capable of disrupting any initiative by activating their agents within the state apparatus.

In addition to 'facts' created on the ground, the settler movement has been building other mechanisms to obstruct future evacuation plans. With the relative success of Habayit Hayehudi in the 2013 elections, and especially in light of this party's success at creating a post-election coalition with Yesh Atid (whether this success is ad hoc or long-lasting is still to be seen) the settler movement has been successful in placing supporters and former leaders in pivotal veto-point positions in both the government and administration. While the successful implementation of these veto points can only be assessed in retrospect – once evacuation is again put on the agenda – the placement of settlement supporters in positions capable of channelling funds and overcoming the bureaucracy seems clear.

In terms of public opinion, the Israeli right has succeeded in two parallel avenues: first, framing the electoral agenda for the 2013 elections and, second, obtaining public support for issues consistent with right-wing ideology. In terms of the former, the overwhelming majority of political parties participating in the 2013 elections completely ignored the Palestinian issue in their campaign messages – an issue which had dominated the Israeli election agenda for decades. Yet in 2013, only three Zionist parties – Hatnuah, Meretz and Kadima – gave the issue a prominent place on their agendas. Together, these parties managed to secure only 11.6% of the votes.

In terms of a broadening public and potential electoral support for issues consistent with right-wing ideology and propaganda, the primary success lies with the ability of Habayit Hayehudi party to position itself firmly within the economic and social agendas of the working and middle class in Israel. In doing so, the party is broadening its potential base for voter mobilization from the territories of the West Bank – its natural and historic stronghold – into central Israel. Examination of voting behaviour in urban voting booths in Tel Aviv, Haifa and Jerusalem shows that the party has been successful – even if still only in small numbers – in extending its constituencies and support far beyond West Bank settlements.

Additionally, within the secular Jewish population, support for Habayit Hayehudi is moving beyond that of lower socio-demographic populations and beginning to be evident among the middle and higher echelons of society and elites – groups previously less inclined to support settler parties. With the additional success of the right-wing religious parties, the voter base for right-wing ideology covers almost all of Israeli society. Moreover, ultra-Orthodox religious parties, which were considered swing voters in the Knesset during the 1980s and 1990s, have developed mobilization tactics and rhetoric ever more consistent with that of the right wing.

To conclude, we believe that the social, electoral and political infrastructure of the Israeli right has not declined and will remain a crucial element in Israeli politics for years to come.

Disclosure statement

No potential conflict of interest was reported by the authors.

Notes on contributors

Arie Perliger is Director of Terrorism Studies at the Combating Terrorism Centre and Associate Professor in the Department of Social Sciences, US Military Academy, West Point.

Eran Zaidise is a Lecturer in the Department of Political Science at the Western Galilee College, and adjunct at the School of Public Health of the University of Haifa, Israel.

Notes

1. Aaron David Miller, "Learning to Live with Bibi," *Foreign Policy*, January 23, 2013, http://www.foreignpolicy.com/articles/2013/01/23/learning_to_live_with_bibi_netanyahu_barack_obama_israel_election.

2. See for example Asher Arian, Michal Shamir, and Raphael Ventura, "Public Opinion and Political Change: Israel and the Intifada," *Comparative Politics* 24, no. 3 (1992): 317–34.

3. Arie Perliger, *Challengers from the Sidelines: Understanding America's Violent Far Right* (West Point, NY: Combating Terrorism Centre, 2013), 13.

4. Koch Koen, "Back to Sarajevo or Beyond Trianon? Some Thoughts on the Problem of Nationalism in Eastern Europe," *Netherlands Journal of Social Sciences* 27, no. 1 (1991): 29–42.

5. Cas Mudde, *Populist Radical Right Parties in Europe* (Cambridge: Cambridge University Press, 2007).

6. Arye Naor, *Erets Yisrael ha-shelemah: emunah u-mediniyut* [Greater Israel: theology and policy] (Haifa: University of Haifa Press and Zemorah-Bitan, 2001); Nadav Shelef, *Evolving Nationalism: Homeland, Identity, and Religion in Israel, 1925–2005* (Ithaca, NY: Cornell University Press, 2010).

7. Paul Hainsworth, "Introduction: The Extreme Right," in *The Politics of The Extreme Right*, ed. Paul Hainsworth (London: Pinter, 2000), 11; Cass Mudde, "Right-wing Extremism Analyzed: A Comparative Analysis of the Ideologies of Three Alleged Right-Wing Extremist Parties (NPD, NDP. CP'86)," *European Journal of Political Research* 27, no. 2 (1995): 203–24.

8. Hans-Georg Betz, "Politics of Resentment: Right-wing Radicalism in West Germany," *Comparative Politics* 23 (1990): 15–60.

9. Ami Pedahzur and Arie Perliger, "An Alternative Approach for Defining the Boundaries of 'Party Families': Examples from the Israeli Extreme Right-Wing Party Scene," *Australian Journal of Political Science* 39, no. 2 (2004): 285–305.

10. Gidi Wiez, "Shelly Yachimovich, Ms. Mainstream," *Haaretz*, August 19, 2011, http://www.haaretz.co.il/misc/1.1374238 (accessed January 1, 2014).

11. Martin Edelman, "The Judicialization of Politics in Israel," *International Political Science Review* 15, no. 2 (1994): 177–86; Ralph Hitchens, "Generals in the Cabinet Room: How the Military Shapes Israeli Policy (Review)," *The Journal of Military History* 71, no. 4 (2007): 1321–2; David Nachmias and Itai Sened, "Governance and Public Policy," *Israel Affairs* 7, no. 4 (2001): 3–20; Udi Lebel, "Civil Society versus Military Sovereignty Cultural, Political, and Operational Aspects," *Armed Forces & Society* 34, no. 1 (2007): 67–89.

12. For a review of these mechanisms see Amy Pedahzur, *The Triumph of Israel's Radical Right* (Oxford: Oxford University Press, 2012).

13. According to the Israeli Bureau of Statistics the Ministry of Tourism invested 785,000 shekels in advertising for tourist sites in the West Bank.

14. This data is publicly available online through the committee website at: http://www. bechirot.gov.il/elections19/eng/home_eng.aspx.
15. For some examples see Asher Arian and Michal Shamir, "Candidates, Parties and Blocs: Israel in the 1990s," *Party Politics* 7, no. 6 (2001): 689–710; Rebecca Kook, Michael Harris, and Gideon Doron, "In the Name of G-D and our Rabbi: The Politics of the Ultra-Orthodox in Israel," *Israel Affairs* 5, no. 1 (1998): 1–18; Yoav Peled, "Towards a Redefinition of Jewish Nationalism in Israel? The Enigma of Shas," *Ethnic and Racial Studies* 21, no. 4 (1998): 703–27; Eitan Schiffman, "The Shas School System in Israel," *Nationalism and Ethnic Politics* 11, no. 1 (2005): 89–124; Gershon Shafir and Yoav Peled, "Citizenship and Stratification in an Ethnic Democracy," *Ethnic and Racial Studies* 21, no.3 (1998): 408–27; Sultan Tepe, "Religious Parties and Democracy: A Comparative Assessment of Israel and Turkey," *Democratization* 12, no. 3 (2005): 283–307; Lilly Weissbrod, "Shas: An Ethnic Religious Party," *Israel Affairs* 9, no. 4 (2003): 79–104.

'Something new begins' – religious Zionism in the 2013 elections: from decline to political recovery

Anat Roth

Independent scholar

Habayit Hayehudi party was one of the most noteworthy phenomena of the general elections held in Israel in 2013. In the 2009 elections the party's main predecessor only won three seats, and polls conducted in the first half of 2012 cast doubt upon its chances of passing the minimum threshold. Defying these predictions, Habayit Hayehudi won 12 seats to become the fourth largest Knesset party. This article's primary claim is that the party's success derived from its leaders' ability to cater to the aspirations and needs ensuing from the traumatic 2005 Gaza disengagement and to replace the feelings of distress and disorientation with a positive momentum.

Habayit Hayehudi (The Jewish Home)[1] party, the joint list of the two religious-Zionist parties, the New National Religious Party (NRP) and Tekuma,[2] was one of the most noteworthy phenomena of the 2013 general elections. Polling conducted in the first half of 2012 cast doubts on the chances of the two parties to pass the minimum threshold of votes for Knesset seats.[3] Nine months later, the unified party had received 12 seats (out of 120) to become the fourth largest party in the Knesset.

The last time the religious-Zionist party attained a similar success was in 1977. In the following elections in 1981, the NRP lost half its seats and has since been unsuccessful in attaining more than six seats. The two exceptions, when the party received nine seats, occurred following a significant period of crisis: the 1996 elections following the assassination of Prime Minister Yitzhak Rabin and the 2006 elections following the Disengagement.

In the 2009 elections, there was an attempt to leverage the success of the 2006 elections by uniting all the religious-Zionist factions (the NRP, Tekuma, Moledet, and Ach'i) into one large party that would facilitate the political realization of the religious Zionists' true demographic weight. However, the move failed; right before the elections the united party splintered, and the remaining factions barely passed the minimum vote threshold. The NRP dropped to just three seats, while the National Union Party[4] received four seats but was powerless in the opposition.[5]

In sharp contrast to its success in the military sphere[6] and in the settlements,[7] in the political sphere, the religious-Zionist movement suffered a long list of failures and has not succeeded in translating its demographic weight into seats in the Knesset. Since the failed struggle against the Disengagement, the religious Zionists' faith in non-parliamentary protest has dropped significantly, creating the feeling that they have no true ability to influence the decision-making process in their own state and so to protect themselves from detrimental government policies.[8]

The 2013 elections and their results created a turning point. The election of Naftali Bennett to the head of Habayit Hayehudi, the primary elections in the party, the clear messages of the party leaders, the expansion of the electorate beyond the sectarian borders of religious Zionism,[9] and the long-awaited unification of the religious-Zionist parties (NRP and Tekuma) created a combined conceptual shift among the religious-Zionist public: they regained their self-confidence, their appreciation of the importance of independent political representation and their faith in the ability to make an impact by engaging in the political arena. MK Uri Orbach, one of the heads of the party and its campaign, explained that the stand-out characteristic of the 2013 elections was 'the excitement that we hadn't seen for years. In this election we weren't hearing popular phrases that were commonplace such as "I cover my nose and vote NRP" ... this time the opportunity is tangible'.[10]

This article presents an historical-cultural analysis of the psychological and political processes that religious Zionism has gone through since the Disengagement. Its primary claim is that Habayit Hayehudi's success derived from the party leaders' ability to provide an answer to the desires that emerged from the traumatic 2005 Gaza disengagement and replace the feelings of desperation with a positive momentum.

Trends and processes in religious Zionism following the Disengagement crisis

From settling West Bank to reinforcing Jewish identity: agenda shift in religious Zionism

From the onset of the settlement movement in the 1970s, the main issue promoted by organized religious Zionism was the Land of Israel. Despite the fact that the founding documentation of Gush Emunim explicitly states that their main goal is 'the strengthening of the Jewish identity',[11] in practice, the lion's share of their efforts were focused on establishing settlements in the West Bank and Gaza. The real agenda shift came in the wake of the Disengagement.

In the midst of the anti-Disengagement struggle and even more so in its wake – faced with the widespread support for Ehud Olmert's 'Realignment Plan' – many religious-Zionist leaders claimed that the willingness to give up land is a result of a crisis of identity in Israeli society, a denial by the secular public of their traditionally Jewish values.[12] This issue became a major topic of discussion among the religious Zionists during the Disengagement, as well as following its execution. Leading up to the 2009 elections, it was actualized in the political platform of the unified religious-Zionist party, stating that 'Jewish education and the deepening of Jewish identity is our utmost national priority'.

Simultaneously, growing numbers of religious Zionists began volunteering for projects aimed at influencing the core values of Israeli society and specifically strengthening the Jewish and Zionist identity of the state and society. For example, there was great demand among graduates of religious girls' high schools to do their national service in 'the Centres for Jewish Identity', which provide Jewish studies classes in secular public schools. Also, the demand for 'Garinim Toraniim' (religiously oriented community-embedded social outreach groups) increased dramatically. Since the Disengagement, these groups have grown both in number and in size.[13] Other examples include the establishment of social movements such as Im Tirtzu, a movement that drew many religious Zionists to its ranks for its work to strengthen the Zionist identity in Israeli academia and culture, and 'Raising the Flag', a movement that organizes values-based activities for the general public, such as candle-lighting ceremonies on Chanukah, dancing with flags in the centre of town on Jerusalem Day,[14] and the like.

The de-legitimization crisis and image-reconstruction efforts

Another outcome of the failed struggle against the Disengagement was the internalization by religious Zionists of the serious damage caused by what was seen as a 'de-legitimization campaign' carried out over the preceding decades against the settlers and settlements in Israeli academia, literature (non-fiction) and media,[15] as well as the understanding that the threatening image that had developed over the years was one of the main factors that led to the eventual failure of the struggle against the Disengagement, the massive support for evacuating settlements and the public apathy towards the evacuees' suffering.[16]

As early as the 1990s, there were those among the religious Zionists who had already began to notice the social erosion of the settlers and settlements in the eyes of the Israeli public and likewise called attention to the need to invest not only in establishing settlements, but in public relations as well. A number of programmatic articles called upon the religious Zionists to 'settle in the hearts' and not only on the hilltops; they likewise called upon the religious-Zionist youth to go work in media.[17] However, the majority of settlers ignored these calls. Influenced by the pioneers of the Labour Movement, of whom they saw themselves as successors, the common perception was that expanding settlements and creating 'facts on the ground' was more important than any public relations effort. Furthermore, the fact that, despite the Oslo Accords, and despite the ongoing negotiations with the Palestinian Authority, the Israeli government had yet to engage in any operative measures to evacuate the settlements gave the settlers a sense of security: that the settlements were an irreversible fact and that the current strategy of mass protests, field work and political lobbying was enough to thwart any future threat to their enterprise. These strategies were applied during the struggle leading up to the Disengagement. However, in contrast to past success, they turned out to be ineffective this time. The governmental systems, headed by shapers of public opinion, worked together to assist Prime Minister Sharon in carrying out the Disengagement, using various methods of de-legitimization to brand the settlers as an extremist violent minority that is endangering Israeli democracy.[18] This systemic cooperation isolated the religious Zionists, generated widespread public support for the Disengagement and enabled Prime Minister Sharon to ignore his own party members as well as the protests of the right.

The implementation of the Disengagement plan undermined the fundamental assumptions previously held by religious Zionists and led to new insights with far-reaching consequences. The first was that the political reality in the West Bank is reversible and that without widespread public support the entire settlement enterprise is in danger. Additionally, trust in the 'traditional' strategies was undermined. The politicians' complete disregard, and foremost that of Prime Minister Sharon, of the mass protests that took place during the Disengagement – the largest of which was attended by 150–250,000 protesters – led to the conclusion that masses heading out to the streets are not as effective as they used to be, especially when they appear sectarian. It was concluded that in order to have an impact on the decision makers, it is necessary to influence public opinion. Lastly, the religious Zionists had become fed up with being perceived as 'the other'. Until the Disengagement, many of the settlers were convinced that the majority of Israelis saw them as their pioneering emissaries and that even though most Israelis did not take an active part in the settlement activity, they nonetheless supported and appreciated their efforts. The sectarian character of the protests against the Disengagement, as well as the public apathy towards the suffering of the evacuees, created a feeling among religious-Zionist circles that the public had not only disengaged from the Gaza Strip, but also from the settlers themselves. 'A large part of our community suddenly realized that the flag that we were waving for years didn't connect to anyone', said Shaul Goldstein, Mayor of the Gush Etzion Municipality and Deputy Chairman of the 'Yesha Council', 'we suddenly understood that we are pioneers leading no camp'.[19] The feeling of loneliness hurt the religious Zionists not only because of the political consequences, but also because of the gap revealed between their self-image and their public image.

In contrast to the threatening and isolationist image that had developed, the religious Zionists, and specifically the 'Torani branch' among them, actually hold a 'Mamlachti' perception,[20] which guides them to full integration in Israeli society, taking part in all areas of social and national achievement, loyalty to the army and state and concern for the unity of the nation and the state. During the

Disengagement period, this Mamlachtic perception was explicitly expressed by the open declaration opposing insubordination and the decisive call for an exclusively non-violent struggle. The de-legitimization campaign against them during the Disengagement period revealed that the general public was not aware of these beliefs. The detachment and alienation from Israeli society felt by religious Zionists created a gap between idea and reality, and this cognitive dissonance led to three types of response: on the one hand, there were calls among some religious Zionists to disconnect from the state, to re-examine their relationship with secular society, to emphasize their sectarian identity and to wear prominent and visible religious identifiers. On the opposite side of the spectrum, there were those who sought to distance themselves from the status of 'the other' by adopting secular practices, a phenomenon already identified by Yair Sheleg in the 1990s,[21] as well as dissemination of the '*Dati Light*' (moderate religious) group,[22] characterized by the suppression of prominent and visible religious identifiers.

The majority of the religious-Zionist community, specifically the youth who went through the Torani education system, was somewhere in between the two abovementioned trends. On the one hand, they have a strong religious-Zionist identity, belief in the path, a feeling of pride and a desire to be a model that others will seek to imitate. On the other hand, they have a desire to cease to be 'the other', 'the religious'. In contrast to the aforementioned trends, the majority of religious Zionists do not feel that there is an inherent contradiction between integration into society and being religious; they believe they can do both. In an attempt to minimize the gap between his all-Israeli self-image and his aloof image among secular society, the new religious Zionist does not change his lifestyle outright, but does distance himself from the sectarian identification by defining himself as 'Israeli'.[23]

This position resulted in a number of practical initiatives, from both organized institutions and private individuals, which through educational and publicity efforts operating to bypass the media, aimed to rehabilitate the negative image of the settlers and settlements and to create empathy and identification in place of apathy and alienation. One of these initiatives was the decision of the 'Yesha Council', the settlers' extra-parliamentary leadership, to establish a public relations department. Its first campaign was launched in 2008 and its aim was to remove the negative image of 'the territories' by emphasizing their cultural and historical importance. Since 2009, the department has been taking shapers of public opinion (usually media personalities) on educational tours in the West Bank, which include meetings with local residents and tours of factories, tourism sites and educational institutions, under the title 'It's about time we get to know West Bank'. A similar project was initiated by the Samaria municipality in 2008 that has since brought over 25,000 visitors to the area, most of whom are policy makers and media personalities. In 2010, the 'Yesha Council' established a research department that produces various papers, pamphlets, maps and other materials to be distributed to the public and to decision makers. Another project started by the 'Yesha Council' was the 'My Israel' movement, which by using new media and social networks succeeding in reaching new audiences and influencing public discourse and decision-making processes.[24] In 2011, another project was launched, called 'Mishkefet – National Acquaintance Project',[25] which organizes tours for the general public throughout the West Bank. Over 1000 tours have been organized since its launch and tens of thousands of people have taken part. The Binyamin and Gush Etzion municipalities have put a special emphasis on developing tourist attractions for the general public, including wineries, hiking trails and historical sites. The 'Regavim' movement, established after the Disengagement by young members of the Tekuma party, created a legal research institution in order to change the territories' international legal status and legitimize the settlements of the West Bank. Even in popular culture there have been noticeable efforts to present the religious Zionists as non-threatening, such as the television programme 'Srugim' about young religious Zionists in Jerusalem and the books *Yesha is Fun* by Karni Eldad (the daughter of former MK, Professor Arieh Eldad) and *Shutter* by Emily Amrusi (former spokeswoman for the 'Yesha Council'). Another expression of this trend is the fact that more young religious Zionists take media studies and make efforts to integrate into media practice and many young settlers choose to move to 'Gar'inim Torani'im' in cities.[26]

Political reorganization: from indirect influence to direct influence

Until the 1977 elections, the NRP was the home party of the religious-Zionist camp. Most of the voters who saw themselves as religious Zionists voted for it and consistently gave it 10–12 seats in the Knesset.[27] In the 1981 elections, the NRP lost half of its seats and, as mentioned previously, up until the most recent elections, did not pass the threshold of six seats. The number of religious Zionists in the Knesset was larger than just the number of NRP members in power because some got elected via other parties, such as 'HaTchiya', 'Morasha', 'Tami', 'Memad' and 'National Union'. However, on the whole, since the 1977 elections, the representation of religious Zionists in the Knesset has been less than their electoral potential. The political weakness was counterbalanced by the 'Yesha Council', the non-parliamentary representation for the settlements, which managed to secure their interests by building cross-party political alliances, especially with the Likud party. Their success in the three decades leading up to the Disengagement led many to view them as one of the most influential political interest groups in Israel,[28] and thus, naturally, it was they who led the struggle against the retreat from Gaza. The failure of the anti-Disengagement struggle not only damaged their stature, but undermined the faith of their people in non-parliamentary struggle in general. The feeling that the entire secular public is suffering from a moral crisis, as well as the harsh disappointment with Likud partners and the ultra-Orthodox parties (who acted against their own public statements), led many in the religious-Zionist community to the conclusion that they can no longer rely on political 'allies', and that they must form an independent political force – first, in order to be influential and, second, in order to develop the ability to lead the country in the future.

This conclusion was already translated into action in the 2006 elections. After the Disengagement, the religious-Zionist political leadership was split into four factions: the NRP, Tekuma, Moledet and Renewed Religious Zionism. Shortly before the elections, in the wake of strong pressure from the religious-Zionist community (led by the religious-Zionist rabbis), the four factions united into one list under the name 'NRP – National Union', which received nine seats in the elections.[29]

Leading up to the 2009 elections, an effort was made to officially unite the factions into one party: under strong pressure from the sectarian media and citizen action groups, the members of Knesset established the unified party under the name Habayit Hayehudi. The goal set by the leadership was to pass the 10-seat threshold. However, the unification did not last and even before the elections the party split into five factions – NRP, Tekuma, Moledet, HaTikva and Ach'i – eventually running in the elections as two lists. The religious-Zionist community was furious over the split and many voters moved their support to other parties, especially Likud. As a result, for the first time in the history of the State of Israel the religious-Zionist community almost lost its political representation entirely: the NRP that ran under the new name Habayit Hayehudi received just three seats in the Knesset and the 'National Union', comprised of 'Tekuma,' 'HaTikva' and 'Our Land of Israel', received four seats.[30]

The four-year term of the 18th Knesset (2009–2013) was characterized by an ongoing argument among religious Zionists regarding the required course of action for the next elections: further efforts towards independent political representation, or integration into the Likud party. On the one hand there was the religious Zionists' long-term desire to become a leading and influential force in and of itself: to wave its own flags, and promote its own values. On the other hand, the religious-Zionist community had completely lost faith in the current leadership. Their behaviour during the Disengagement period, the endless disputes that led to the five 'shrapnel' parties, the break-up of the unified party in which so much hope had been invested and the fact that even after the crushing defeat in the elections, the leaders were still unable to work together broke the public's faith in their leadership altogether and undermined their belief in the chance of establishing their own independent political representation. The discourse taking place in the religious-Zionist media since the Disengagement made it clear that the essential condition for bringing the religious-Zionist voters 'back home' and for translating the sector's true demographic weight into political power was uniting the Habayit Hayehudi and 'National Union' parties. Furthermore, since the 2009 failure, the claim that without unification religious Zionism would lose its political representation was being voiced more strongly. The representatives of the religious-Zionist community in the Knesset were not only seen as ego-driven politicians utterly lacking any and all ability to attract public support, but as the true obstacle to the necessary unification into a single party. The religious Zionists want to become a large, non-sectarian party, explained Rabbi Shlomo Aviner,

> however, our feeling is that the current political leadership is unable to lead the nation, and the proof is, that they can't even lead themselves. The proof is, they split into two parties, and each of the two parties is itself divided. The people say, with deep sadness, and even with a degree of pain: it's a disgrace and an embarrassment.[31]

The continuation of the infighting, which only created pessimism towards the chance of unity, the political and diplomatic challenges and the success of five young, well-spoken religious in winning seats in the Knesset through the Likud party, all made the option of integration into the Likud party seem like the preferable option. MK Moshe Feiglin, a settler from Samaria who began working in this direction back in 1999, claimed as early as the Disengagement period that if the settlers want to prevent another Disengagement, they have no choice but to abandon the 'old sectarianism', to register as members of the Likud party, to vote settlers into the Likud party organs (central committee, secretariat, etc.), and thus to influence from within: 'What's going to decide the future of Israel is not the size of some small parties, but rather the identity of the Likud party leader and the internal balance of power inside the party.'[32] Four years later, faced with the reality that there is no real alternative, Feiglin's strategy became the leading one, and during the years 2009–2010, a mass registration began of religious Zionists joining the Likud party, including many mayors from West Bank municipalities. Thanks to these efforts, the settlers were successful in introducing many of their people to the Likud central committee, having an impact on the party list and advancing those loyal to their cause. Additionally, the political power that the West Bank mayors gained in the party assisted them in advancing their municipalities' interests and in acquiring necessary budgetary allocations from the ministers in the Likud party. Another factor that gave the impression that the integration strategy was the most effective was the fact Prime Minister Netanyahu surrounded himself with religious-Zionist staff members. Beyond the sectarian pride felt by religious Zionists, this process opened a direct line of communication between their non-parliamentary leadership and the prime minister, which assisted greatly in solving various issues.

Nonetheless, many in the religious-Zionist community still felt that the integration into the Likud party is just the lesser of two evils and though they certainly welcomed the advancement from the position of 'kosher supervisor' of the train to the position of 'drivers' assistant', they still held on to the dream of actually having their hand on the wheel. In addition to this psychological aspect, a number of events took place that enraged the religious-Zionist community – such as Netanyahu's Bar-Ilan Speech,[33] the settlements freeze and the evacuations of the Migron settlement and of the Ulpana neighbourhood in the Beit El settlement. All these together brought the religious-Zionist community back to the Disengagement experience and back to the conclusion that it cannot rely on the

Likud. The community's internal discourse focused again and again on the fact that although the nationalist parliamentarians in the Likud had indeed succeeded in a few individual areas, they have no substantial impact on the more fundamental subjects. The Prime Minister only really cares about those who have the ability to topple his coalition, claimed MK Uri Ariel, and therefore if the religious Zionists want to have influence, they must 'unite the forces' and build 'a strong religious bloc that no government can allow itself to ignore or abandon'.[34]

The 2013 elections – something new begins

In April of 2012, after three years of infighting, Habayit Hayehudi announced that it was opening up the party to new members who wished to register and that at the end of the registration period, the party would hold primary elections for both the party list and party chairman. This was the first time in the history of the religious-Zionist party that the people were given the chance to choose their representatives and shape their party list. However, at the outset, it seemed like the step was taken just a little too late. The party's image was at an all-time low, no serious candidate was running and people felt like 'there's nobody to vote for'. Therefore, despite the dramatic announcement, most people remained apathetic. According to polls from that period, the party was not expected to pass the minimum vote threshold.[35]

Eight months later, the party captured the hearts of the religious Zionists and achieved an impressive 12 seats in the elections. As we shall see, the main cause of the leaders' success was rooted in their ability to provide an answer to the aspirations and needs that the religious-Zionist community has developed since the Disengagement. The steps they took, coupled with external factors such as the media and other parties, gave many in the religious-Zionist circles the feeling that 'Something New Begins' – the election slogan chosen by Bennett – that the political and social standing of the religious Zionists is about to change radically and that they are going to become a central, influential power in the State of Israel.

Primaries – renewing the party ranks and rebranding

Looking back, the primaries were the main cause of the transformation of Habayit Hayehudi into an attractive and identifiable party. However, as stated, the change was not immediate. In light of past disappointments, the public did not rush to register for the primaries, and polls from one month after registration opened indicated an average of 3.1 seats in the Knesset.

The first signs of change appeared on 22 May 2012, when Naftali Bennett, former Director General of the 'Yesha Council', and Ayelet Shaked, head of 'My Israel', officially joined the race (Bennett for the position of chairman, and Shaked for the party list). MK Uri Orbach, who was the one who convinced them to run, quickly announced that 'something new is happening',[36] and indeed the very next day a wave of people started registering with the party. The first to enter the race were Binyamin Regional Council Deputy Mayor, Colonel (Res.) Moti Yogev, and chairman of the religious-Zionist youth organization 'Raananim', Major (Res.) Yoni Chetboun (who both announced their support for Bennett). Shortly thereafter they were joined by Shuli Mualem, Jeremy Gimpel and Avi Vurtzman – all young, accomplished individuals well integrated into Israeli society.

The new candidates created an opportunity to renew the party list and change the old guard for some new blood, and in doing so to rebrand the party. The tired, grey, sectarian party, as the old NRP was perceived, was replaced with a young, non-sectarian, proud Israeli party seeking to lead the nation.

Another change of pace brought about by the primaries was unified leadership, in which the members have each other's support. In sharp contrast to the standard Israeli politics, Bennett did not run a personal campaign. Upon entering the race, he presented himself as part of a team, together with Shaked and Orbach (who ran for the party list) and former Israel Defence Forces (IDF) Chief Rabbi Avi Ronksy (who was a partner from outside the party), saying that in order to bring the change, he needs them to be by his side. Later on, Moti Yogev, Yoni Chetboun and Avi Vurtzman joined the team. Against the backdrop of the endless bickering and infighting characteristic of the older leadership, the camaraderie of Bennett and his young team captivated many, strengthened the feeling of change and garnered public support.

The competition between the candidates, the hundreds of meetings around the country, and the intense campaign led by Bennett to encourage people to join the party and vote, which included mass advertising in the sectarian media, social media and an active e-mail list – caused the religious-Zionist street to wake up, successfully convinced people that they have the power to take part and have an impact and led to a massive registration of 54,000 new party members, which was about half the total number of votes the party received in 2009.

On 6 November 2012, Bennett defeated the incumbent Zevulun Orlev, who represented the old leadership, and became the chairman of Habayit Hayehudi. One week later, the party list was chosen: former MK Nissan Slomiansky came in first, and after him Ayelet Shaked, MK Uri Orbach, Avi Vurtzman, Moti Yogev, Yoni Chetboun, Shuli Mualem and Jeremy Gimpel. Multiple studies show the decisive role that the party head plays,[37] and as we shall see, Bennett's election was a key factor in the appeal of the party. Yet the positioning of Slomiansky and Shaked at the top of the list had a major impact as well. Slomiansky's victory placated the veteran NRP activists and supporters – who, according to the results of the 2009 elections, were worth about three and a half seats – some of whom feared that the new party head, together with a new party list, were turning the NRP into a second Likud.

On the other hand, the introduction of a secular woman, Shaked, who received the second highest number of votes,[38] expressed the change in the party image: the willingness of the party to open its doors to new audiences and more specifically the religious Zionists' understanding, as stressed by Bennett again and again, that if they expect traditional and secular Zionists to see Habayit Hayehudi as their political home, they must prove to them that they are real partners who can not only vote, but be voted for as well.[39] Furthermore, Shaked's top position gave the volunteers a feeling that they had something to offer and increased secular identification with the party. Some of the notable expressions of this included the mock elections held on university campuses,[40] as well as the Mina Tzemach survey held one month before the elections, which showed that a third of the Habayit Hayehudi votes came from secular or traditional voters.[41] The party's success at crossing the sectarian boundaries created much excitement among the religious Zionists. 'The fact that so many people are talking about us' affects not only the polling, but 'more importantly impacts the mood in our community', claimed MK Uri Orbach. 'Suddenly, so many people are realizing that political power doesn't only impact budgets and laws, but also the way a young religious-Zionist perceives his place in society.'[42] Since the party opened its doors to secular Zionists, Habayit Hayehudi became 'everyone's leading party', added *Besheva* editor Emmanuel Shilo. 'The religious-Zionist community now has an opportunity to rise from the dust and turn its disagreeable, disgraced political representation into a victorious political force that cannot be ignored. We will not miss this opportunity.'[43]

In the 'Tekuma' party, which joined the Habayit Hayehudi party a month and a half before the elections, though they did not have open primaries, the central committee members who created the party list did not ignore the public demand for renewing the party list: with the exception of veteran MK Uri Ariel heading the list, the rest of the candidates were new to the list, yet familiar faces in religious-Zionist circles: Rabbi Eli Ben-Dahan, Zevulun Kalfa, Orit Struk, Rabbi Hillel Horvitz and Nachi Eyal.

The joint party headed by Naftali Bennett managed to preserve a balance of power between the two parties, mixing veteran politicians with new faces, young and old, men and women, secular and religious, Ashkenazi with Sephardic, and relayed a message of renewal, openness and vitality.

Bennett's messages

Naftali Bennett's messages touched the heart of the transformations that religious Zionism underwent following the Disengagement. As opposed to his opponents, who emphasized the sectarian identity and their duty to protect sectarian interests, Bennett spoke of national leadership and turning Habayit Hayehudi into a big, non-sectarian party, that would take responsibility for all Israelis and shape the character of the state: 'The goal is to connect the entire Jewish-Zionist people in Israel under one umbrella organization' and to turn Habayit Hayehudi into a political home for

anyone who longs for a state with a clear Jewish-Zionist identity, and [for anyone] ready to take responsibility for more than their own basic individual needs ... not only observant Jews ... our community is not only religious. It's all-Israeli. Religious Israeli, Zionist Israeli, Israeli who takes responsibility for the state – on issues of diplomacy, society, economics, and education.[44]

'The time has come to go out and make an impact. As it is, we're already doing so in every field.'[45]

Though Bennett did begin his campaign with a diplomatic plan, at the centre of which was his opposition to the Palestinian state and his suggestion to annex Area C to Israel,[46] the Israeli–Palestinian conflict played a minor role in his campaign. The main goals put forth by Bennett were strengthening Jewish-Zionist identity – 'to bring back the State of Israel's Jewish soul'[47] – and turning religious Zionism into a leading, impactful and central political force that cannot be ignored. Alongside his call for opening the doors to wider audiences, Bennett also cultivated pride among the religious Zionists: at every turn he would emphasize their contribution to the country and their advantage versus other parties. 'In Shas they only see holiness in Torah, the Likud-Beitenu only see the importance of the state ... we are the only party that sanctifies both the Torah and the State of Israel.'[48] Therefore, explained Bennett, religious Zionism must 'assume command':

> Stop with the 'sector' issue, go out to the people of Israel as a whole, in the public domain as well ... our people know how to be the leaders in every field: in the IDF command, in the education system, in the Gar'inim around the country, in the charity organizations. Only in one place we're not taken seriously – the Knesset. In the political arena, for some reason, we're spending all day dealing with errands and deals ... instead of being the leaders, we've turned into the religious-affairs NCO's[49] of Israeli politics. This is how we are perceived by the Israeli public, by the other parties, and by the Prime Minister. He takes us for granted.[50]

Another aspect of Bennett's messages was their sharpness and clarity. Despite the efforts to reach new audiences, Bennett did not dampen his messages or blur his ideology. His harsh criticism of the justice system, his explicit opposition to a Palestinian state, his open call to annex the West Bank, his refusal to uproot settlements,[51] and his talk of the need for religious Zionism to inherit the leadership from secular Zionism in order to base life in the State of Israel on Jewish values[52] altogether captivated the youth and generated much excitement among the religious Zionists.[53]

Bennett's image: charisma, youthfulness, biography and an all-Israeli icon

One of the most influential factors in the religious Zionists' deep identification with the Habayit Hayehudi party was Bennett's image. The primary component in this image that swept the public, especially the youth, was his charisma, his ability to speak with any audience in their terms and his infectious excitement and faith. The second component was his youth. For young people who were disappointed in the older generation that had previously led them, 40-year-old Bennett was not only something new, but was perceived as 'one of us'.

Furthermore, he succeeded in turning to the youth by communicating in their language and with their tools: text messages, active e-mail and primarily Facebook. One of the more outstanding examples of his youthful style was his decision to begin public appearances with the phrase 'my brothers and sisters' – a phrase that eventually became his logo (and a hit among the youth). Additionally, Bennett personally sent constant updates from his campaign journey via e-mail and Facebook, instilling the youth with a feeling of closeness, heightened by his use of simple, informal language.

The third component was his personal biography. He was a combat officer,[54] having served in elite special-forces units, was the CEO of a successful high-tech company that sold for millions of dollars, was Netanyahu's former chief of staff, served as director general of the 'Yesha Council' and established 'My Israel'. All these accomplishments made Bennett a symbol of leadership, excellence and success – an image that many young people sought to imitate. Additionally, due to the fact that he was representing the antithesis of the politicians and political dealers that the public had grown sick of, he became a favoured alternative for those who sought leadership from the public service sector and a model of identification for the 'silent bourgeois majority' of the religious Zionists.[55]

The fourth component was the perception of Bennett as an all-Israeli icon: a religious man, proud of his association with religious Zionism, holding solid right-wing views, unafraid of expressing his desire to annex the West Bank, unapologetic about criticizing the government, while simultaneously success-fully reaching significant positions of power in the secular world and being honoured and respected by both the secular elite and the average person on the street. Bennett was fully aware of his own success, and during his campaign he stressed the fact that he was never considered 'the religious guy. Our basic identity, for all of us, is Jewish-Zionist'.[56] This model of a proud religious Zionist, who achieves success in the secular world without giving up his values, without giving up his unique identity, all the while expressing his own views without those surrounding him labelling him as 'the other', 'crazy' or 'an enemy', captivated many religious Zionists, especially among the Torani communities.

Simultaneously, even though Bennett presented strong right-wing views, he nonetheless was considered an attractive candidate even among the 'lightly religious' and 'socially religious' – those who associate themselves with the religious-Zionist community even though they only partially observe the religious commandments. Their behaviour often deviates from the boundaries of what is considered permissible according to Jewish law and their outward religious identifiers are often the minimum required.[57] This community never felt comfortable among the Torani religious Zionists and never saw itself voting for the 'National Union' party, whose leaders and a great part of its supporters are perceived to be very judgemental.[58] They had a much easier time identifying with Bennett, a resident of Raanana, an upper-middle-class mixed (religious/secular) town, who married a secular woman and looks altogether secular (despite the small skullcap on his head), does not speak in messianic terms, emphasizes the

Jewish-Zionist basis that unifies religious and secular (as opposed to isolationist religiosity), believes in partnering with secular society and works emphatically at advancing these principles. His position at the top of the list, coupled with his support among the Torani communities, was taken by the 'religious-light' communities as a sign of their legitimacy as well; and thus it enabled them to vote for a list of which most of the representatives are Torani.

Unity in the ranks

Another factor that brought hope and excitement to religious Zionism and increased support for Habayit Hayehudi was the merger with the 'National Union' party. The yearning for unity among the ranks was felt already during the primary elections and appeared in almost every candidate's campaign, including Bennett's.

After the primaries, there were loud calls from the religious-Zionist circles for a unification of the parties: 'Don't miss the hour', said the mayor of the Hebron Mountain Regional Council, don't calculate 'who's worth more' or 'who'll lead', just sign! This move 'will bring home tens of thousands of voters who left to seek political relevance elsewhere'. It is in your hands whether 'religious Zionism takes off or crashes'.[59] The Secretary General of the 'Tekuma' party said: 'There is only one thing that every single candidate from both parties promised – unity and running together, and now is the time to fulfil [this promise].'[60]

On 29 November 2012, the chairmen of the two parties kept their promise, signed a unification agreement and announced: 'something new begins with unity between us'. The feeling of 'togetherness' that for the first time in years enabled the religious-Zionist community to work together generated immense excitement on the ground and many believed that, as was written in the end-of-campaign advert: 'Now we can make history. This time we can be part of the national leadership, we can be great in the public arena as we have been in other areas of life, and we can be who we truly are. This time it's possible.'

Steps and trends influenced by external factors

The awakening of the religious-Zionist street and the rallying of the religious Zionists behind Habayit Hayehudi was influenced by the mainstream media as well as the other political parties, whose behaviour actually increased the support for the party and strengthened the feeling that indeed 'something new begins'.

One of the factors was the decision of the Likud and Yisrael Beitenu parties to run on a joint list, which caused many religious-Zionist voters to return to Habayit Hayehudi. Primarily, the unification made Likud–Yisrael Beitenu the biggest party, so many religious Zionists who wanted Netanyahu to become prime minister assumed that his victory was secured and therefore felt free to vote for Habayit Hayehudi.[61] Also, many religious Zionists were uncomfortable with the secular Yisrael Beitenu party.[62] Additionally, these new circumstances made Habayit Hayehudi the only party to the right of Likud with a chance of getting into the Knesset and therefore the only choice for those who sought to strengthen Netanyahu from the right. These considerations helped the party to rise in the polls, and as MK Nissan Slomiansky explained: 'Once the public sees that you're successful, that there's a chance to have an impact, that you could get a lot of seats in the Knesset, people say to themselves, "something has happened. This isn't a niche party anymore. This is a serious party"'.[63]

A second factor that greatly helped the rise of Habait Hayehudi in the polls was Netanyahu's personal assault on Bennett. A month before the elections, Bennett was interviewed on TV Channel 2 and said that if he were given the order to evacuate a Jew from his home, his conscience would not allow him to do it and he would ask his officer to exempt him from the mission. Although he clarified that he would not publicly call for insubordination, the leaders of the Likud party headed by Netanyahu pounced on the opportunity to present him as an irresponsible leader, willing to hurt the IDF and undermine the rule of law. However, the assault only helped Bennett and strengthened Habayit Hayehudi party, which rose in the polls from an estimated average of 11.85 seats to 13.30 in just one week. Beyond the empathy towards Bennett,[64] the personal attack against him gave the impression that Netanyahu saw Bennett as a threat. This gave the religious Zionists the feeling that their leader was a realistic candidate able to take Netanyahu's place as prime minister.

A third factor was the campaign against Habayit Hayehudi. After the attempt to damage Bennett's image failed, the Likud began attacking his party: when speaking to secular voters, they argued that behind Bennett's pretty image hides a list of backwards extremists who blindly follow rabbis' orders and added that Yigal Amir, the man who assassinated Prime Minister Rabin, supports the party. When speaking to religious Zionists, the main argument of the Likud campaign was that Habayit Hayehudi is putting them in the sectarian category,[65] adding that the only way to have a real impact is to join the Likud party. In addition to the work done by the religious-Zionist representatives in the Likud list, Netanyahu got the mayors of the municipalities in the West Bank to sign a letter of support for the Likud–Beitenu party, which emphasized the importance of voting for a leading party.

The letter was advertised in all the sectarian media outlets for weeks, but the religious Zionists paid no heed. Since their representatives in the Likud party were elected to the top of the party list and their seats in the Knesset were pretty much guaranteed, the potential 'Likud Beitenu' voters felt no need to give it their vote. The main reason, though, that many religious-Zionist voters abandoned the Likud in favour of Habayit Hayehudi was the aggressive de-legitimization campaign that the Likud led against it. Not only because they saw the religious-Zionist party as the Likud's natural political partner, but because the campaign cast doubt upon the religious Zionists' loyalty to the State of Israel. 'You're well aware that this is exactly the nasty tactic that was used against you in the beginning of your career', Bennett pointed out to Netanyahu; 'for years they tried to paint you as a dangerous extremist. And now, you're trying to do the same thing to us, the religious-Zionists'.[66]

A fourth factor was the media attention that Bennett received in Israel and around the world.[67] The fact that almost every article about the polls leading up to the election focused on the increasing support for Habayit Hayehudi coupled with the increasing media coverage of Naftali Bennett's successes in garnering support from secular Israelis, Israeli youth and Likud supporters, not only accelerated these trends but also inflated the feeling of pride among the religious Zionists and the feeling that something new *is* beginning – that religious Zionism is indeed becoming a relevant, significant political force that cannot be ignored.

The fifth factor that assisted the collective rallying behind Habayit Hayehudi was the lack of argument regarding the peace process. Since the peace deal with Egypt, the topic of territorial compromise was one of the core issues preventing political unity among the religious Zionists. In the 2013 elections, for the first time in three decades, the territorial issue was considered irrelevant. The lack of peace talks and the loss of faith among the Israeli public regarding the chances of ever reaching an agreement created a basis for cooperation among the factions. 'Everyone knows that there's no serious partner on the other side', explained Rabbi Aharon Lichtenstein to the leaders of Meimad party, 'and therefore the issue of hawks and doves is not actually an issue … today, there is no practical meaning to the peace process issue, so we should just work together on the other issues that everyone can agree on.' If we want 'to be able to serve the people of Israel in love and faith', then we have to become a large party, and therefore we are obligated 'to go to the voting booths and vote for Habayit Hayehudi. No one can be absent'.[68]

Conclusion

An analysis of the results of the 2013 elections reveals that among the supporters of the Habayit Hayehudi party are about six Knesset seats worth of new supporters compared to 2009. Even if half of them are secular Israelis as Asher Cohen claims,[69] the 2013 elections clearly point to a trend of 'coming home'. It is difficult to measure at this stage if the party will succeed in living up to the high hopes of its voters, how it will change the stature of religious Zionism – both in its own eyes and in the eyes of others – and whether or not it will one day become the leading party. These questions are largely dependent on the actions of the party leaders in the years to come and more importantly how it is perceived by the public. What can be said at this stage is that the last election strengthened the religious-Zionist communities, moving them from the political periphery to the centre of attention, enhanced certain social developments, brought them to political power, and rebranded the religious-Zionist party as an all-Israeli, victorious, valued, modern and young party.

For the first time since the Disengagement, the religious Zionists hold their head high. The primaries, the unification of the parties, the mixed and representative party list, the leaders' identity, the messages they carried and the reaction of the political system – all these rehabilitated the religious Zionists' faith in their political leadership, in politics as a whole and in their ability to impact on the political process; and gave them the feeling that something new and good is beginning. They were given the feeling that they can succeed in the political arena, that they are no longer reliant on the kindness of others, that they can no longer be ignored, that the public at large is beginning to recognize the gap between their threatening public image and reality and, as shown in various polls, many are willing to translate their positive feelings towards the religious Zionists into voting for them. Finally, the success of breaching the sectarian boundaries has made the dream of leading the state look possible and reachable. The pact between Bennett and Lapid[70] during the assembling of the coalition and their success in forcing Netanyahu into a coalition on their terms, including their coalition demands, only added to these feelings and to the overall faith of the religious Zionists in their political leadership.

Disclosure statement

No potential conflict of interest was reported by the author.

Notes on contributor

Anat Roth (PhD) is an Israel-based independent scholar and author of two books on Israeli politics.

Notes

1. In Hebrew, the name of the party contains the definitive article. In order to reduce confusion, throughout the article the name will be treated in English as if it is not defined.
2. Lit. revival or uprising.
3. Iynon Shalom, "Dahaf Institute Survey: The NRP and National Union Parties – Out of the Knesset," *Srugim website*, April 30, 2012, http://www.srugim.co.il/31429-%D7%A8%D7%A2%D7%99%D7%93%D7%AA-%D7%90%D7%93%D7%9E%D7%94-%D7%A1%D7%A7%D7%A8-%D7%9E%D7%9B%D7%95%D7%9F-%D7%93%D7%97%D7%A3-%D7%A7%D7%95%D7%91%D7%A2-%D7%94%D7%9E%D7%A4%D7%93%D7%9C-%D7%9C%D7%9C%D7%90-%D7%A0?di=1 (accessed January 1, 2014).
4. Between the 2006 and 2009 elections, the 'National Union' Party consisted of 'Tekuma', 'Ach'i' and 'Moledet', and except for MK Aryeh Eldad, all the other representatives of this party were religious Zionists. After the failed unification attempt with the NRP, the list changed, and the three parties that now made up the 'National Union' Party were 'Tekuma', a religious-Zionist party, 'HaTikva', the secular-nationalist party of Aryeh Eldad, and 'Eretz Yisrael Shelanu', a party made up of pupils of Rabbi Meir Kahane and Messianic Chabad Hassidim led by Rabbi Shalom Dov Wolpo ('HaTikva' means 'The Hope' and 'Eretz Yisrael Shelanu' means 'Our Land of Israel').

5. Asher Cohen and Bernard Susser, "Stability in the Haredi Camp and Upheavals in Nationalist Zionism: An Analysis of the Religious Parties in the 2009 Elections," *Israel Affairs* 16, no. 1 (2010): 82–104.

6. Yagil Levy, *The Other Army of Israel: Materialist Militarism in Israel* [in Hebrew] (Tel Aviv: Yediot Ahronot and Sifrei Hemed, 2003); Reuven Gal, ed., *Between the Yarmulke and the Beret – Religion, Politics and Army in Israel* [in Hebrew] (Ben Shemen: Modan, 2012).

7. Akiva Eldar and Edith Zertal, *The Lords of the Land: The Settlers and the State of Israel 1967–2004* [in Hebrew] (Or Yehuda: Dvir, 2004).

8. Settlers Talk, "Let's Take Responsibility on our Future" (paper presented at conference held at Matte Binyamin, January 26, 2006).

9. Asher Cohen, "Something New Begins: The Transformation of the Religious-Zionists in the 2013 Elections – From an Open Party Camp to Multiple-Party Representation" [in Hebrew], in *The Elections in Israel 2013*, ed. Michal Shamir (Jerusalem: The Israeli Democracy Institute, forthcoming).

10. Uri Orbach, "Worried There May be Optimism," *Besheva*, December 16, 2012.

11. "Gush Emunim: A Movement for the Rejuvenation of Zionist Fulfillment" (an early Gush Emunim pamphlet, n.d. [1974]), 1.

12. For example: Rabbi Zvi Tau, *Those Who Hope in God, Will Renew Their Strength* (Jerusalem: For Eye to Eye They See, 2005); Rabbi Zvi Tau, *And They Shall Face One Another*, A Collection of Religious Articles about the Activity of the Panim-el-Panim Organization (2005); Rabbi Zvi Tau, *Our Path in This Time*, Principles of Religious-Zionist Rabbis (2006).

13. Elyashiv Reichner, *There of All Places – The Story of the Social Settlers* [in Hebrew] (Tel Aviv: Yediot Sfarim, 2013).

14. The day commemorating Israel's victory in the 1967 War.

15. Anat Roth, *Not at Any Cost – From Gush Katif to Amona: The Story behind the Struggle over the Land of Israel* (Tel Aviv: Yediot Sfarim, 2014), 30–41; Anat Roth, "Theories of Fundamentalism versus Reality Test: The Torani-Stream of Religious-Zionism and its Struggles against the Disengagement Plan and the Destruction of Houses in Amona" [in Hebrew] (PhD diss., Bar Ilan University, 2011), 12–19; Udi Lebel, "'The Disengagement': An Attempt at Elite Exchange in the IDF and in the Israeli Society" [in Hebrew], in *In the Shadow of the Disengagement: Strategic Dialogue in Crisis*, ed. Haim Misgav and Udi Lebel (Jerusalem: Carmel and the Academic College of Netanya, 2008), 207–32; Eli Avraham, *Behind Media Marginality – Coverage of Social Groups and Places in the Israeli Press* (Lanham, MD: Lexington Books, 2003); Eithan Orkibi, "Judea and Samaria in Israeli Documentary Cinema: Displacement, Oriental Space and the Cultural Construction of Colonized Landscapes," *Israel Affairs* 21, no. 3 (2015): forthcoming.

16. Roth, "Theories of Fundamentalism," 237–8; 229–30.

17. Uri Orbach, "The Good to Media" [in Hebrew], *Nekuda* 106 (January 1997): 12–13. In Hebrew, the title plays off a well-known phrase calling on the best youth to join the Paratroopers Brigade.

18. Lebel, "The Disengagement"; Roth, *Not at Any Cost*, 230-267; Roth, "Theories of Fundamentalism," 100–127.

19. Meiron Rapoport, "Shaul's Lamentation," *Haaretz*, December 8, 2005.

20. The Torani Branch relates to the students and successors of Rabbis Kook. For more information about their 'Mamlachtic Perception' see Roth, *Not at Any Cost*, 43–84; Roth, "Theories of Fundamentalism," 33–59.

21. Yair Sheleg, *The New Religious* [in Hebrew] (Jerusalem: Keter, 2000), 54–93.

22. Rav Shagar, *Tablets and Broken Tablets* [in Hebrew] (Tel Aviv: Yediot Sfarim and Rav Shagar Institute, 2013), 373.
23. Yonah Goodman, "Enough (Nullifying) the National Religious Sector" [in Hebrew], *Be'Ayin Hinuchit* 123 (April 2013). It stands to reason that this process was greatly helped by the development of the Torani Pre-Army Preparation ('Mechina') Programs. For further information about the 'Mechina' Programmes see: Elisheva Rosman-Stollman, "Religion and the Military as Greedy Frameworks: Religious Zionism and the Israel Defense Forces" (PhD diss., Bar-Ilan University, 2005), 148–71.
24. As of April 2013, 'My Israel' is one of the largest social media groups in Israel with over 100,000 members.
25. Mishkefet means binoculars in Hebrew.
26. Reichner, *There of All Places.*
27. Asher Cohen, "Religious Zionism and the National Religious Party in the 2003 Elections: An Attempt to Respond to the Challenge of Religious, Ethnic and Political Schism," in *The Elections in Israel 2003*, ed. Asher Arian and Michal Shamir (New Brunswick, NJ: Transaction, 2005), 187–213.
28. Anat Roth, *The Secret of its Strength: The Yesha Council and its Campaign Against the Security Fence and the Disengagement Plan* [in Hebrew] (Jerusalem: The Israel Democracy Institute, 2005).
29. Asher Cohen, "The Religious Parties in the 2006 Elections," *Israel Affairs* 13, no. 2 (2007): 325–45.
30. Asher Cohen, "The Splintered Camp: Religious Zionist Parties in the 2009 Elections," in *The Elections in Israel 2009* (see note 27), 69–92.
31. Rav Shlomo Aviner, "An All-Israeli Party," *Be'Ahava Ube'Emuna*, June 1, 2012.
32. Moshe Feiglin, "The Knesset Moved to the Likud Central Committee," *Besheva*, September 29, 2005.
33. June 2009, where he committed to the two-state solution.
34. Uri Ariel, "Don't Wait for the Primaries," *Makor Rishon*, May 4, 2012.
35. Shalom, "Dachaf Institute Survey."
36. Uri Orbach, "When a Truly Successful Candidate Comes from Outside (the Party), I'm Willing to Give Up (my Seat)," *Besheva*, May 24, 2012.
37. Ofer Kenig, "Election and Dismissal of Party Chairmen: Israel, a Comparative Study" [in Hebrew], in *Candidate Selection in Israel: Reality and Ideal*, ed. Gideon Rahat (Tel Aviv: The Institute for the Study of Society and Economics in Israel, 2006), 37–58.
38. In one-third of the settlements in Judea and Samaria where voting booths were set up, Shaked received the majority of the votes. In the more Torani settlements, like Alon Moreh and Eli, she gained the highest score.
39. Naftali Bennett, "No More Camps – Working Together to Be in the Next Government," *Besheva*, November 8, 2012; Dvora Ginsburg, "Bennett and Orlev – Decision Time," *Besheva*, November 1, 2012.
40. At the Hebrew University Campus the Habayit Hayehudi received 16.4% of the votes, at Tel Aviv University 8%, at Sapir College 23.3% and at the Interdisciplinary Centre in Herzliya 18.3%.
41. News Broadcast, *Channel 2* (Israel), December 18, 2012.
42. Orbach, "Worried There May be Optimism."
43. Emmanuel Shilo, "The Force to the Right of Netanyahu," *Besheva*, January 17, 2013.
44. Naftali Bennett, "Assuming Command," *Besheva*, May 24, 2012.
45. Naftali Bennett, Election advertisement: "Taking Command, Registering!" (June 2012).

46. Naftali Bennett, *The Israel Stability Initiative: A Practical Outline for Israeli–Palestinian Conflict Management*, February 2012.
47. Naftali Bennett, "We're Going to Go Back to Being a Political Force," *Makor Rishon*, November 2, 2012.
48. Bennett, "No More Camps."
49. Refers to low-ranking non-commissioned officers in the IDF charged with seeing to it that the religious soldiers' ritual needs are met
50. Bennett, "Assuming Command."
51. See television interview with Nissim Mishal in "Mash'al Cham," *Channel 2* (December 20, 2012). As a result of intense public criticism following the interview, Bennett backed down from his previous statement, and clarified that he would request that his commander exempt him from the mission, though he would not directly refuse orders.
52. Ari Shavit, "The Story of the Success of Bennett, the Failure of the Left," *Haaretz*, December 28, 2012.
53. Avichai Boaron, "B is Bait Leumi," *Maaynei Ha'Yeshua*, November 24, 2012.
54. Being a combat soldier in the IDF is perceived in Israel at large, and among the religious Zionists in particular, as the ultimate symbol of Zionism and "Yisraeliyut" (being Israeli), and contributes greatly to the popularity of Israeli leaders vying for public support. A strong example is Ehud Barak's political campaign. (Ben Caspit and Ilan Kfir, *Ehud Barak: Israel's Number 1 Soldier* [in Hebrew] (Tel Aviv: Alpha, 1998).) Likewise, this isn't the first time the NRP has been led by a former combat officer with the hope that this would lead to increased popularity. In 2002, the NRP was led by Brigadier General (Res.) Efi Eitam. Bennett's advantage lay in his combination of qualities.
55. Asher Cohen, "Religion and Patriotism between Acceptance and Opposition: Shattered Visions in Religious-Zionism" [in Hebrew], in *Patriotism: Homeland Love*, ed. Avner Ben-Amos and Daniel Bar-Tal (Tel Aviv: Dionun and Hakibutz HaMeuchad, 2004), 468. For a discussion on the impact of economic status on the political participation of the religious Zionists see: Nissim Leon, "The Secret of its Weakness: The Religious Zionism versus the Disengagement Plan" [in Hebrew], in *In the Shadow of the Disengagement: Strategic Dialogue in Crisis*, ed. Haim Misgav and Udi Lebel (Jerusalem: Carmel and the Academic College of Netanya, 2008), 269–84; Nissim Leon, "Religion, Social Class and Political Action of the Religious Zionism in Israel" [in Hebrew], *Democratic Culture* 12 (2009): 105–44.
56. Bennett, "Assuming Command."
57. Asher Cohen, "The Crocheted Skullcap and What it Represents: Multiple Identities in Religious-Zionism" [in Hebrew], *Akadamot* 15 (2004): 24–5.
58. Efrat Shapira-Rozenberg, "Don't Call Me 'Torani,'" *Ynet*, February 4, 2009, http://www.ynet.co.il/articles/0,7340,L-3666727,00.html (accessed January 1, 2014).
59. Tzviki Bar-Chai, "One Camp, One Flag," *Makor Rishon*, November 16, 2012.
60. Nachi Eyal, "The True Moment of the Religious Zionism," *Me'at Min Ha'Or*, November 23, 2012.
61. Cohen, "Something New Begins."
62. Ibid.
63. MK Nissan Slomiansky, Interview (April 9, 2013).
64. Cohen, "Something New Begins."
65. The highlight of the de-legitimization campaign was a series of advertisements paid for by Likud activists in which Bennett is seen behind barbed wire next to the caption "The Jewish Ghetto headed by Bennett".
66. Hazki Ezra, "Bennett to Netanyahu: Your are Responsible for the Disgraceful Clip," INN, October 10, 2013, http://www.inn.co.il/News/News.aspx/249791 (accessed September 1, 2014).

67. "Naftali Bennett, Israel's New Rightwing Star," *France 24*, December 25, 2012; David Remnick, "The Party Faithful," *New Yorker*, January 16, 2013; Nick Meo, "Israel's New Political Star Naftali Bennett's Jewish Home Party Determined to Stop Palestinian State,' *Telegraph*, January 19, 2013.
68. Menachem Rahat, "The Unifying in the 'HaBayit HaYehudi' is Greater than the Dividing," *Matzav Ha'Ruach*, January 18, 2013.
69. Cohen, "Something New Begins."
70. Head of the secular party 'Yesh Atid'.

An uneasy stability: the Haredi parties' emergency campaign for the 2013 elections

Nissim Leon

Department of Sociology and Anthropology, Bar-Ilan University, Ramat-Gan, Israel

This article examines the emergency election campaign launched by the Haredi parties in anticipation of the 2013 general elections in Israel, in order to attract the votes of those generally perceived as their automatic supporters – the Haredim. The 2013 campaign was a struggle for the 'converted' – the Haredi vote – amongst UTJ and Shas supporters alike. The battle was fought openly and assertively. The intensive efforts ultimately achieved what may be described as an uneasy electoral stability. The reasons for this situation, and how the Haredi parties addressed it, is the subject of this article.

This article examines the emergency election campaign launched by the Haredi parties in anticipation of the 2013 general elections in Israel with a view to attracting the votes of those generally perceived as their automatic supporters – the Haredim.

Over the past four decades, elections in Israel have generally been opportunities for a show of force by the Haredi parties. Voter turnout in Haredi areas has been high, with almost universal ideological loyalty to the centrist Haredi parties – the Sefardi Shas party and the Ashkenazi United Torah Judaism (UTJ) (Yahadut ha-Torah) party. Their campaigns aimed to broaden their electorate, appealing to voters outside of the Haredi sector. Shas was successful in this endeavour, establishing its power base with voters who were, in many cases, not themselves Haredim. United Torah Judaism was less successful in this regard. The vast majority of the party's voters are Haredim. While Shas could rely on the religious influence of its rabbis on Mizrahi[1] traditionalists[2] as well as on active religious outreach,[3] UTJ relied mainly on the demographic growth of Haredi society.

In the run-up to the 2013 general elections, something seemed to be going wrong. Trends of change that had appeared in the first years of the previous decade had now hardened into facts. First of all, Haredi society had grown. However, this demographic growth did not necessarily mean increased power. Growth had brought diversity and a multitude of internal challenges. For instance, a significant rise in the number of children in Haredi families was accompanied by a permanent state of deprivation – which could be accommodated ideologically but bore the seeds of unspoken protest, with frustration at the inability of the politicians representing Haredi society to provide for its everyday needs.

Secondly, Haredi society has witnessed a mushrooming of various ideological models of everyday life, at both the individual and family levels. At the same time the ideological framework and the educational system representing them has broadcast a conflicting conservative message. This chasm has produced two kinds of responses: confusion, apathy and political defiance on one hand, and support for more conservative, fundamentalist trends on the other.

In both instances, Haredi society has been re-examining its boundaries, its principles and its political and ideological tradition. It is this restless reality that was encountered in the 2013 campaign by Haredi party activists such as the field coordinators, advertising professionals, survey analysts and politicians. The result was a frenetic campaign whose focus turned from an attempt to reach outward to new voters back to securing the core.

The 2013 campaign, then, was a struggle for the 'converted' – the Haredi vote – amongst UTJ and Shas supporters alike. This battle was fought openly and assertively. The vote count indicated rather limited achievements. Shas managed to increase its absolute support in relation to the previous elections, but in an election campaign with a high percentage of votes in areas supporting centre-left secular parties, this was not manifest. The number of Shas seats in the Knesset remained at 11. United Torah Judaism increased its representation slightly, from six MKs to seven, but this merely served to regain ground lost since the 1988 elections.

Other parties that competed openly for the Haredi vote, including the list led by Rabbi Haim Amsalem and that led by Rabbi Amnon Yitzhak, failed to pass the electoral threshold. Amsalem's list earned 42,450 votes, while Yitzhak's list garnered 26,368. Together, these two lists attracted 68,818 votes, while the electoral threshold – the minimum number of votes needed for a party to enter the Knesset – stood in the 2013 elections at 73,000.

What the intensive efforts ultimately achieved might be described as an uneasy electoral stability. The reasons for this situation and how the Haredi parties addressed it will be the subject of our discussion.

The Haredi parties and the 2013 elections

The complex attitude of Haredi society towards Zionism and the State of Israel is characterized by two ideological trends. On one side there are the extremist groups that distance themselves from any open, official partnership with the state.[4] On the other side, there are those who might be referred to as the Haredi 'mainstream', who recognize the state and its leaders and are willing to take an active part in political life. The mainstream, representing the great majority of

Haredi society, has been led for more than two decades by two parties: United Torah Judaism and Shas.

United Torah Judaism is a reincarnation of the Agudath Yisrael party, which was established in Poland in 1912. Its voters are mostly Ashkenazi Haredim. Shas is an ethno-Haredi party founded in Israel in 1984. Since its establishment, it has been the political home of the families of Sefardi yeshiva students and of the traditionally observant Mizrahi public. While UTJ maintains an outspokenly sectarian political approach, Shas permits itself a broader, more nationally minded perspective.[5] As noted, Shas was distinctive in its diverse voter base, including both Haredim and non-Haredim.[6] This helped to consolidate the party's position as the largest religious party in Israel.

United Torah Judaism is comprised of two factions. The first is the veteran Agudath Yisrael, affiliated today with the Hassidic communities, especially the dominant Gur Hassidic group. The other faction is the relatively newer Degel ha-Torah, founded in 1988, representing the 'Lithuanian' yeshiva population. Each faction has a spiritual leadership body organized as a guiding council, but over the past 40 years both the Lithuanian and Sefardi streams of Haredi society have become accustomed to a sort of papal model of absolute subservience to a single accepted authority.[7]

The Agudath Yisrael faction follows the guidance of the heads of the major Hassidic groups, such as Gur and Vizhnitz. Amongst Degel ha-Torah members, much attention has been focused over the past year on Rabbi Aharon Leib Steinman, the 98-year-old head of a Bnei Brak yeshiva.

Shas is officially led by a 'Council of Sages', but actual control of the party since its establishment has rested in the hands of 92-year old Rabbi Ovadia Yosef, one of the leading halakhic authorities in contemporary Judaism and a former Chief Rabbi of Israel. These elections were the last political campaign that Rabbi Ovadia led. In 22 October 2013, 10 months after the elections, Rabbi Ovadia passed away. Shalom Cohen (born 1931), a strict Rabbi and the head of Porat-Yossef yeshiva, was promoted to be the official chief of the 'Council of Sages' of Shas.

Since the political upheaval of 1977, the Haredi parties have exerted great efforts in creating alliances with the ruling parties and serving in the government coalition.[8] This is vital for the simple reason of the degree to which Haredi society is dependent on the government: it is a society in constant demographic growth, existing as an insular group which – by choice – is not fully integrated in the workforce, and is therefore reliant on the mechanisms of the welfare state, as well as enjoying a de facto exemption from compulsory military service.

The Likud–Yisrael Beiteinu electoral alliance, announced at the start of the 2013 election campaign, made it clear that Benjamin Netanyahu would head the next government. From this point onwards, parties viewing themselves as potential Likud-led coalition partners intensified their campaigning efforts, in anticipation of future negotiations with the ruling party. Prominent among these were the Haredi parties.[9] As part of their efforts to ensure their place once more as a significant force within the coalition, they sought to increase their electoral power and hence their negotiating position.

At first, UTJ and Shas tried to overcome their sectoral image and appealed to non-Haredi audiences. United Torah Judaism presented itself as having achieved social benefits not only for Haredi society, but also for the lower socio-economic strata and for the country's geographical periphery. Shas, in a controversial campaign, presented itself as the guardian of the ethnic boundaries of the Jewish nation in Israel.[10] Both parties promised to protect the weaker strata from the economic decrees that were expected to follow the elections in view of the necessary cuts to the state budget. However, what became increasingly clear was that the main campaigning target was the home front – Haredi society itself – which seemed quite apathetic to what was going on.

Some interviewees told me that this was the usual pattern in a Haredi election campaign: it always started slowly, with participation growing and reaching a peak by the end. However, this time the Haredi parties put special effort into filling what seemed to be real cracks in the usual voting bloc. These cracks, indicating a possible drop in the number of Knesset seats, fanned the fear of abstentions – not to mention a trickle of votes to other parties. Field activists reported not only apathy but also a sort of protest on the part of loyal voters towards the Haredi parties.[11] One even described the situation to me as the 'Haredi winter protest'.[12]

It was clear that Haredi society was no longer composed solely of closed, obedient communities of religious scholars. For nearly a decade, Haredi society in Israel has been involved in a process of diversification of lifestyle. Increasing numbers of Haredi families are integrating into the workforce; increasing numbers of Haredi men are performing military or civilian national service, and effectively dropping out of the yeshiva world.

There are thus more and more intermediate elements that are willing to contemplate a different, more open Haredi lifestyle. Another aspect of this change relates to the internet revolution. While the recognized Haredi rabbinical leadership had been successful in making TV taboo, the internet front is a battle they are losing. For various reasons which lie beyond the scope of our present discussion, the internet has come to occupy an important place in Haredi society, bringing exposure to social and political information and criticism that does not always sit well with the accepted ideological guidelines. This is easily discerned even on Haredi news websites. These provide not only reporting on and documentation of Haredi society, but also biting social and political criticism that is directed both outwardly and inwardly. Quite often, the targets of this criticism are the Haredi politicians.

This reality in flux can go in two opposite directions:[13] One is a distancing from traditional voting patterns, whether in the form of abstention or of voting for non-Haredi parties. The other direction is a desire on the part of conservative elements to restore the former state of affairs. The first trend has not yet produced any significant organization on the countrywide level. The second has led to the appearance of a new conservative party under the leadership of Rabbi Shmuel Auerbach. The context of this development will be clarified below.

Another scenario that concerned Haredi politicians was the possible weakening of Shas. This party's ability, over the years, to mobilize non-Haredi voters helped the Haredi parties in general to present a broad Haredi front on matters of principle, such as the question of mandatory army enlistment for men. This time, Shas found itself confronting defiance, protest and criticism from within the ranks, presenting a genuine threat to its stability. The reasons for this opposition related mainly to the party's division of power and accessibility to decision-making positions.

This was not the first time that problems of this kind were cited as the reason for candidates leaving the fold of Shas and running – unsuccessfully – on separate lists: this scene had been played out in 1992 with a list led by Yitzhak Peretz; in 1999 a separatist group was led by Rabbi Yosef Azran; and the family of Rabbi Yitzhak Kadouri made a similar attempt in 2006. This time, however, the separatists demonstrated actual organizational and mobilizing ability, and their criticism was sharp and resounding both on account of their media skills and because general society showed an interest – whether ideological, as in the case of Haim Amsalem's party, or diversionary, as in the case of the colourful preacher Amnon Yitzhak.

Schism: the conservative rupture in UTJ

The 2013 UTJ election campaign started off with a severe ideological rupture in its Lithuanian faction, Degel ha-Torah. This rupture had appeared with the death of the faction's elderly leader, Rabbi Yosef Shalom Elyashiv, and the ensuing battle over its spiritual leadership. The struggle was conducted between loyalists of Rabbi Aharon Steinman, the 98-year-old Bnei Brak Rosh Yeshiva, who had been regarded for many years as the second-most important leader amongst the Lithuanian Haredi sector, and the followers of Rabbi Shmuel Auerbach, the 86-year-old conservative Jerusalemite halakhic authority.

The battle over the succession heated up as the election campaign got underway, with the financial seizure by Rabbi Steinman's supporters of the *Yated Ne'eman* newspaper, which serves as the ideological mouthpiece of the Degel ha-Torah party.[14] The newspaper had long been a source of attacks on and criticism of Rabbi Steinman. Its editors preferred Rabbi Auerbach. The move resembled the takeover of a TV or radio station by revolutionaries. Rabbi Auerbach's supporters responded by starting up a new ideological paper, *Ha-Peles*. This was countered by Rabbi Auerbach's representative being left off the Degel ha-Torah list for the Knesset. The result was the establishment of Rabbi Auerbach's new Lithuanian Haredi list – Netzah.

The battle between the Lithuanian factions concerned more than just the division of power and prestige. The respective leaders represent opposing approaches to the 'Israelization' revolution that has been quietly unfolding amongst Haredi society.[15] Its most prominent manifestation is a growing move, by men and women alike, into the job market, and the sprouting of numerous professional courses and academic institutions adapted to Haredi requirements. While Steinman is perceived as being willing to condone this change, so long as loyalty is maintained towards the spiritual leadership and the fundamental communal frameworks, Rabbi Auerbach is perceived as rejecting any deviation from the Haredi way of life as consolidated over the decades.[16] The intervention of the Rebbe of Gur, promising that UTJ would oppose any change in the Haredi lifestyle, allowed Auerbach to finalize the party list and instruct his loyalists to vote for UTJ.

What concerned the UTJ rabbis and strategists alike was the fact that votes for the Netzah party – even in very low numbers – could diminish UTJ's power at what seemed to be a critical time in the relations between political forces, in view of the budgetary and civil measures that the new government was likely to adopt.

Now, less than a month before elections, UTJ addressed itself to fighting what it believed to be its voters' apathy, and what turned out to be the prospect of a possible trickle of Haredi votes to other parties. Activists explained this prospect to me as reflecting bitterness on the part of the regular UTJ voters over the lack of solutions to routine problems.

One of the most pressing of these problems concerned registration for Haredi educational institutions. The number of existing schools does not meet the growing need, and especially amongst the more prestigious institutions there is a sense that parents apply year after year to register their children, but encounter a selection system characterized by nepotism and prejudice. The inability of the political leadership to solve this problem, experienced by so many of its constituents, was openly and prominently featured in Haredi public discourse, arousing much criticism of and resentment towards Haredi politics and politicians.

Heterodoxy: the shake-up of Shas

The shake-up of Shas started with the reappearance of the party's former political leader, Aryeh Deri. He hinted at the possibility of establishing a competing party, and his persuasion of the spiritual leadership that only he could restore the party to its former strength led to his reappointment. To avoid offending Eli Yishai, Minister of the Interior and head of the Shas party list for more than a decade, it was decided that the Shas campaign would be led by a troika consisting of Deri, Yishai and the Shas Minister of Housing Ariel Attias.

Some observers expected this arrangement to hinder the running of the election campaign. The troika managed to focus on the task at hand, but the ungainliness of its operations made itself felt. Apparently, this was not only the result of tension between the personalities involved,[17] but also due to the extreme deference that each was careful to demonstrate towards the others. In any event, the top Shas figures very quickly discovered that the main problem was not just the challenge of managing the campaign and mobilizing the regular voters, but rather the separatist trends, which became apparent following the appearance of two lists headed by leaders familiar to the Mizrahi Haredi public. The first was the Am Shalem party, headed by former Shas MK Rabbi Haim Amsalem. The second was the Koah Lehashpi'a party, headed by the charismatic religious outreach preacher, Amnon Yitzhak.

Amsalem, a Shas MK, had been removed from the party at the instruction of the religious leadership after he publicly expressed his objection to what he perceived as the Sefardi party's submissiveness to the spiritual leadership of the Ashkenazi Haredi parties. Amsalem's one-man faction in the Knesset became a vocal opposition to Shas policy. His criticism focused on Shas' subservience to Ashkenazi Haredim and the discrepancy between what he described as traditionally moderate Sefardi religiousness, connected to the real world, and the model of the scholar society and the culture of religious stringency currently fostered by the spiritual leadership.[18] Amsalem built the essence of his campaign around ideological principles which were receiving prominent attention in the public discourse in Israel – especially criticism of the inequality in the burden of military service. Amsalem did not merely use memorable slogans; he set forth his arguments in notices and publications attacking Haredi politicians, with an emphasis on Shas.

The story of Amnon Yitzhak was different. Yitzhak is one of the most prominent and most veteran of the religious outreach preachers in Israel.[19] His attempts, in recent years, to rejuvenate the charisma of his organization found expression in purist campaigns decrying changes within Haredi society. These campaigns received a generally cool reception amongst the Haredi spiritual leadership, who were willing to view Yitzhak as a talented evangelist, but not as a guardian or standard-bearer of Haredi society. His attempts to obtain Rabbi Steinman's backing for his activities received a rather vague response. His attempts to reach Rabbi Ovadia Yosef were likewise rebuffed. Like Amsalem, Yitzhak did not hesitate to level the accusation that the spiritual leader of Shas was surrounded by a small and self-serving group. Like Amsalem, he too put together a Knesset list whose purpose was to outdo Shas. The agenda of the new party, 'Koah Lehashpi'a – under the guidance of Rabbenu [our teacher] Amnon Yitzhak',[20] competed directly with that of Shas in its support for the poor and in promoting the lowering of the cost of living in Israel.[21]

While Amsalem was viewed as an ideological challenge who could be dismissed as a troublemaking heretic, Yitzhak turned out to be mainly a psychological challenge. The symbolic reputation that he had accumulated over the course of his prominent outreach work turned the Koah Lehashpi'a party into an electoral enigma for Shas. Yitzhak emerged from the fluid sphere of the religious outreach industry. His audiences were in fact the same public upon which Shas had built its electoral stability over the years: the newly observant and those in the process of becoming more observant.[22] If, in the past, Amnon Yitzhak's propaganda machine had warned that tens of thousands of newly observant Jews would change the demographic balance in Israel, this time Yitzhak spoke of the tens of thousands of newly observant Jews who were loyal to the authority who had shown them the true path: Amnon Yitzhak. The same propaganda machine which in the past had rebuffed messages of de-legitimization aimed at Shas now stood confronting the party itself, ready to combat any attempt at de-legitimization aimed against Yitzhak.[23] Therefore, the working assumption of the Shas activists was that Yitzhak might take a significant bite out of their reservoir of voters.

In the meantime, Yitzhak and his criticism of Shas became a media story that was receiving Israeli prime time coverage.[24] The level of concern amongst Shas leaders rose in view of Yitzhak's repeated public declarations that he had conducted secret polls revealing his true strength. The political system in Israel has become accustomed to relatively small or unknown parties demonstrating surprising shows of strength in elections. Shas itself was an example, in 1999. The Pensioners party was another example, in 2003. Yitzhak tried to present his party in the same light.

Shas invested considerable energy to combat both Amsalem and Yitzhak. Its activists followed Amsalem to the local meetings he would organize, decrying him as a traitor. His books were burned by unnamed elements. Amsalem, who had considered himself the representative of the legendary Abuhatzeira family of kabbalists among Shas supporters, was confronted with an open letter written by Rabbi David Abuhatzeira, urging exclusive support for Shas.[25] Yitzhak suffered similar treatment. His public gatherings were disrupted by Shas supporters using heavy-handed violence. Excommunication notices were distributed against him in Haredi neighbourhoods. Above all, there was the public complaint by Rabbi Ovadia Yosef, a week before the elections, to the effect that Yitzhak was persecuting him and his family. A mild stroke that Rabbi Ovadia suffered prior to the elections was explained by activists as the result of his anguish over home-grown opponents of Shas.

The emergency campaign

The last fortnight of the Haredi election campaign was dominated by a direct appeal to the Haredi public. The aim was to remind them of the boundaries of Haredi society and of its fundamental principles. We shall refer to this strategy as 'taboo politics'. In addition, the election campaign that had originally been intended as an outwardly oriented showcasing of the principles of Haredi society became a campaign explaining Haredi society to itself. This strategy will be referred to as 'totem politics'.

Taboo politics

At the core of 'taboo politics' we find an emphasis on the threats perceived by Haredi society as having the power to change its essential character. In the 2013 elections, two such subjects featured on the emergency campaign agenda: military conscription and Haredi education.

In general, while the majority of the Jewish population in Israel enlists and performs mandatory military service, Haredi women are exempt and enlistment is postponed for students of Haredi yeshivot. Israeli law bars these scholars from either working or acquiring an education or professional training unless they can produce an exemption from military service. Thus, young Haredi men are distanced from any horizon of social mobility on an individual basis, which is the middle-class pattern in modern nation-states. The result is that Haredi society in Israel has become, in the words of Menachem Friedman, a 'scholar society' – i.e. a society that rests upon a broad moratorium on conscription and on participation in the labour market for men, who are engaged instead in religious studies.[26]

Over the past 40 years, the scholar-society model has become a central principle in Haredi society. Haredi leaders argue that traditional religious study in yeshiva frameworks is not only the foundation of Haredi life, but has also played a role in the spiritual maintenance of the entire Jewish nation and the state. While the Haredim and their leaders claim to have no problem with the enlistment of those who leave the yeshiva for the army, they imply that anyone who deviates from the Haredi model is in fact deviating from the core values of Haredi society.

The demand to cancel the postponement of military service for Haredi yeshiva students and to advance a universal enlistment law occupied a prominent place in the public discourse in Israel leading up to the 2013 elections. Foremost in the public's mind was the episode of the broad government which the Likud had formed, with some urgency, with Kadima in the summer of 2012. Its aim had been to settle this question of military enlistment legislation. Differences of opinion on the matter led to the dissolution of the government and triggered early elections. The Yesh Atid party, led by Yair Lapid, advocated compulsory military or civilian national service for all and gathered immense support amongst the secular middle class in Israel.

It then became easy for the Haredi parties to emphasize that Haredi society was now facing a real threat. The taboo of recruitment of yeshiva students was about to be broken. In gatherings of UTJ activists, which addressed mainly yeshiva students, propagandists spoke of a difficult time for Haredi Jewry. Army enlistment was presented as a decree which, without Haredi political power and without a general mobilization of the Haredi camp, would be transformed from theory into reality. Yeshiva students would be removed from the yeshivot by force of the law, and compelled to enter the army. A symbolic expression of this threat was demonstrated on election day itself: tens of thousands of call-up orders arrived by mail in Haredi neighbourhoods. Obviously, these were dispatched not by the army but rather by the UTJ party headquarters.

This was not the only threat emphasized in the emergency campaign. United Torah Judaism argued that another taboo was about to be broken – the autonomous status of the Haredi educational system. Secular forces were described as ready to use their growing political power to force unsupervised study materials onto Haredi schools and yeshivot. It might have been clear that this could not be done by force, but what the secular forces might do, the Haredi parties argued, was to raise obstacles for Haredi education and harm it through withholding funds and through direct intervention in curricula. The political efforts of many years were about to go down the drain.

As an example, one of the notices that was distributed in Haredi neighbourhoods described what would happen the day after elections: Haredi children would now, on the instructions of the secular Ministry of Education, be forced to study names and concepts from secular culture at the expense of their study of Torah and Jewish tradition. Outside of Haredi society this threat may be difficult to understand, but within the society there is broad agreement that where traditional education is concerned, full autonomy must be maintained. A general education may be important and useful, but only after the child has grown up, studied Torah in a suitable framework, married, and is ready to find a way to support himself and his family.

Thus, the strategy of 'taboo politics' played on the fear of the imminent threat of the state intervening in the Haredi way of life. It played on the balance between the desire of the Haredim to integrate into Israeli society and their desire for cultural autonomy. The Haredi parties reminded their constituents that even in an age of integration, the Haredi parties were there to protect Haredi tradition. This strategy was profoundly effective among yeshiva students.

Totem politics

Anthropologists describe a totem as a creative object inspired by animals or plants and aimed at representing a certain tribe or person as an example of a spiritual leader. In a similar manner, spiritual leadership that enjoys universal admiration does not remain an icon, but becomes a totem; from the point of view of society, that leadership is its central representative.

One of the conspicuous developments in contemporary Haredi society is the convergence around rabbinical figures who are admired, imitated and clung to. The ideological expression of this trend is reflected in the expression '*da'at Torah*' (the 'Torah view') – the ideological justification for the public to relinquish its power and leave decisions in all areas in the hands of the rabbinical leadership.[27] The cultural expression of the same trend is the iconization of these figures who are referred to as 'the *gedolim*' ('great ones').[28]

It is easy to view the admiration of the Haredi spiritual leadership – especially venerable rabbis in their 80s and 90s – as a totem culture which reflects a consensus that the public is able to rally around, even in a situation of flux and crisis. Indeed, such an elderly leadership, in the absence of any organized mechanism of succession, invites an atmosphere of uncertainty. The lack of clarity with regard to these rabbis' messages, their indistinct speech, physical frailty and measured pace all contribute to the symbolic rather than operative role of the leadership, a situation which does not necessarily foster a sense of stability.

On the other hand, these rabbinical figures are imbued with greater symbolic weight. The aged leadership, seen as so close already to the upper worlds, is perceived as being above all controversy, and for this reason its pronouncements are received as if they were the words of the living God.

In the final week of the campaign, the elections were depicted not only as a show of Haredi determination in the face of the anticipated threats, but also as a vote of confidence in the respected spiritual leadership. Haredi websites, which usually have no compunction in criticizing the political leadership, were adept at translating and proclaiming the message of support for the spiritual leadership. A banner on one of the popular Haredi news sites read, 'Hold your nose and vote for Maran [our master]'. In the background, surrounding the words 'Hold your nose', photographs of the party's bigwigs were shown in hues of grey. Under the words 'vote for Maran' there appeared a colour photograph of Rabbi Aharon Leib Steinman, spiritual leader of the Lithuanian sector of Haredi society. Similarly, Shas bigwigs reminded its pool of regular voters that theirs was not just another party: it is the life project of the man they admire most – Rabbi Ovadia Yosef. In residential areas identified as strongly supportive of Shas, notices were displayed describing Rabbi Ovadia Yosef weeping over voter apathy. His son, Moshe, is quoted on one poster as saying: 'I got up at 3 a.m. to check that everything was okay. I saw my father praying, weeping, and asking God: Don't allow the enemies of Israel to uproot my whole life's work.'[29] A huge billboard was displayed at the entrance to the Haredi city of Bnei Brak, with the inscription: 'We love the Holy One, blessed be He, and vote for Rabbi Yosef, God's emissary.' Among the people I interviewed, some viewed this election as a sort of gesture of respect for a world that had once been. Others viewed it as a renewal of a covenant with the past.

Conclusion

The taboo and totem strategies were successful. Amsalem's list failed to cross the electoral threshold, as did Yitzhak's party. The UTJ campaign was undertaken with noticeable fervour. A student at a Lithuanian-style yeshiva in Kiryat Malakhi told me:

> The Rosh Yeshiva spoke to us several times during the week before the elections, slamming his Gemara shut and announcing that presently an emergency was occurring, and every possible voter must be mobilized to vote for UTJ, otherwise we'd all end up in the army. During the week before the elections, my yeshiva friends and I made hundreds of phone calls – to parents, distant cousins, whoever, just so they'd vote UTJ.

Residents of Modi'in Ilit described UTJ activists campaigning almost door-to-door. The aim was not to neglect a single potential voter.

The sociological and political uncertainty concerning what was going to happen led to an assertive psychological rescue campaign. It included, on the one hand, intimidation linked to the possible fate of Haredi society following the elections (taboo politics) and, on the other hand, a mobilization to defend the honour of the elderly spiritual leadership (totem politics). The results show that psychology trumped sociology (once again, but only for the time being). The price paid was that of electoral stability in a state of unease, both during the campaign and afterwards.

Data from the various voting stations showed that in Haredi cities such as Modi'in Ilit, Beitar Ilit and Elad, Shas retained its strength, while UTJ grew slightly stronger. Voter turnout remained more or less what it had been in the 2009 elections – 85–90%. Interestingly, in Modi'in Ilit and Beitar Ilit, both Haredi cities devoid of any non-Haredi residents, 5–10% of voters supported non-Haredi parties. This represented an increase of 100% in relation to the same phenomenon in the 2009 elections.[30]

Some view the Chabad and Breslov Hassidic groups as having been responsible for giving an extra Knesset seat to the UTJ party. This cannot be asserted with any certainty. In Kfar Chabad, for example – the location most closely associated with Chabad hassidism in Israel – only 699 votes were cast for UTJ, with 103 for Shas, while 1278 voters preferred the extreme right-wing party, Otzma le-Yisrael, continuing the Chabad trend of voting for such parties. As to the contribution of Breslov Hassidim, the picture is not clear-cut. Firstly, there is no single group of Breslov Hassidim. Groups calling themselves Breslov Hassidim are spread throughout Israel under the guidance of different leaders. One location that may give some indication as to their voting patterns is the rural settlement of Yavne'el in the Galilee. Most of its residents are secular, but a community of one of the Breslov groups resides there too, which would logically indicate that the votes within Yavne'el for Haredi parties would come from this group. However, the Yavne'el voting record shows that 705 votes were cast for Shas and only 33 for UTJ.

Ultimately, the 2013 elections were defined by the profound changes the Haredi society is undergoing following more than a decade of restlessness.[31] The Haredi voter dutifully gave his vote, in most cases, to the Haredi parties. But anyone paying attention to the Haredi streets during the elections could not ignore the general sense of dissatisfaction with this option. The fear of army enlistment, or the commitment and loyalty to the rabbinical leadership, may have helped to mould the 2013 elections, but so did another important element: the social protest of the summer of 2011, which led tens of thousands of Israelis onto the streets to protest at the cost of living, to demand equality in bearing the national burden and to denounce the politicians. The protest found its voice in the 2013 elections in the prominence awarded to the economic and civic messages of the Labour party, Yesh Atid and Bayit Yehudi campaigns. It ultimately led to Yesh Atid becoming second in number of Knesset seats. Interestingly, though, the social protest also found a voice in Haredi society.

One of the prominent features of the 2011 summer protest was the absence of Haredim. They shied away for various different reasons: the protesters' profile, the anti-Haredi sentiments that were occasionally expressed and the nature of the protest itself, which was too 'spontaneous' and popular for a society accustomed to institutionalized political activity. Nevertheless, it turned out that the Haredim simply expressed their protest differently.

The general feeling of being fed up with politics found expression in the Haredi sector in the growing restlessness and internal criticism of Haredi politicians. As amongst the general population, the everyday problems confronting Haredi households seemed to loom larger than the great, ideological questions of principle. However, the Haredi protest did not take the form of demonstrations. It became manifest in the dissatisfaction with the prospect of voting for the Haredi parties, and the need to be wooed by them.

Thus, the emergency campaign might have been successful in slowing down the trend of suppressed protest among Haredi society, but it was not enough. The 2013 elections caught the Haredi parties in a position of weakness. This was reflected in the lack of certainty as to whether they would be 'natural' coalition partners. The Haredi parties were seen as potentially offering stability for a government seeking to renew the political process vis-à-vis the Palestinians, but were also viewed as a profound civic problem arousing instability in the political system as a whole. That which in the past had been taken almost for granted – the fixed model of Haredi votes for Haredi parties – was now something that had to be fought for. While the Israeli general elections ended for the middle class with an exclamation mark, where Haredi society is concerned, they ended with a resounding question mark.

Notes on contributor

Nissim Leon is Senior Lecturer in the Department of Sociology and Anthropology at Bar-Ilan University.

Disclosure statement

No potential conflict of interest was reported by the author.

Notes

1. Jews whose families came from North Africa and Western Asia have been referred to by different terms: Sephardim, edot ha-mizrah, Mizrahim and Arab Jews. Each term expresses a scholarly attitude which takes into consideration the history and sociology of these Jews and their encounter with Israeli society. For convenience, I use Mizrahim, Mizrahi Jews, and Jews from Islamic countries. These terms are clearly biased. Many so-called Mizrahi Jews prefer to use other terms, such as Sephardim, edot ha-mizrah, or have a specific mention of a region or country of origin. Nevertheless, the terms Mizrahim and Mizrahi Jews are widely used to simplify the discussion of issues pertaining to these Jews.
2. In Israel, Jewish religious identity is commonly categorized into three groups: Haredi, religious and traditional. (Each of these groups includes a wide religious and ideological spectrum; the following brief characterizations are therefore very general.) Being 'Haredi' in Israel means belonging to a society which maintains a

separatist religious ideology that is wary of Zionism, committed to the ideal of mandatory Torah study for males and is meticulously observant of halakha (Jewish law). 'Religious' in Israel refers, in most cases, to 'national religious' (or 'religious-Zionist') circles, which are committed to observance of halakha, maintain religious frameworks suited to their nationalist ideological approach, and have a lifestyle oriented toward social integration. To be 'traditional' in Israel means that while a person may not be fully observant of halakha and perhaps not even send his children to a religious school, he nevertheless believes in God and regards halakha as the code for proper Jewish religious practice.

3. David Lehmann and Batia Siebzehner, *Remaking Israeli Judaism: The Challenge of Shas* (London: Hurst, 2006).

4. Kimmy Caplan, "Hitpat'hutam shel Maagalei Hibadlut Bekerev Haredim Kanaim: Amram Blau Kemikreh Mivhan" [in Hebrew], *Tzion* 76, no. 2 (2011): 179–218.

5. Yoav Peled, "Towards a Redefinition of Jewish Nationalism in Israel? The Enigma of Shas," *Ethnic and Racial Studies* 21, no. 4 (1998): 703–27.

6. Ephraim Yuchtman-Yaar and Tamar Hermann, "Shas: The Haredi-Dovish Image in a Changing Reality," *Israel Studies* 5, no. 2 (2000): 32–77.

7. Benjamin Brown, "Orthodox Judaism," in *The Blackwell Companion to Judaism*, ed. Jacob Neusner and Alan Avery-Peck (Malden, MA: Blackwell, 2000), 311–33.

8. Nissim Leon, "The After-Shocks of the 1977 Political 'Upheaval' and their Role in the Rise of Shas" [in Hebrew], *Israel – History, Society, Culture* 15 (2009): 1–32.

9. This article represents an initial summary of the findings of intensive field work carried out during the election campaign (December 2012–January 2013) among Haredi party activists, including MKs, paid activists, yeshiva students and party candidates. The work included interviews, gathering of written and filmed materials, participation at conferences, and exposure to Haredi newspapers and websites. All of these sources served to clarify the general mood and direction.

10. See, for example, http://www.youtube.com/watch?v=7U8EP8egvE0 (accessed January 1, 2014).

11. Interview with Eli Malka, Shas activist, in the south of the country, January 3, 2013.

12. Yehuda Winnet, UTJ activist in Jerusalem, interview, January 5, 2013.

13. Nurit Stadler, *Yeshiva Fundamentalism: Piety, Gender and Resistance in the Ultra-Orthodox World* (New York: New York University Press, 2009).

14. David Erlanger, "Orekh Hapeles, Nati Grossman Nidkar Berosho Baknisa Leveito," *Shtiebel*, December 21, 2012.

15. Kimmy Caplan, *Internal Popular Discourse in Israeli Haredi Society* [in Hebrew] (Jerusalem: Zalman Shazar Centre for Jewish Studies, 2007), 94–138.

16. Asher Atedgi, "Between Bnei-Brak and Jerusalem," *Makor Rishon*, August 10, 2012.

17. Yishai Cohen, "Because of an Election Poster," *Kikar Hashabbat*, December 1, 2012, http://www.kikarhashabat.co.il/%D7%91%D7%92%D7%9C%D7%9C-%D7%A9%D7%9C%D7%98-%D7%91%D7%97%D7%99%D7%A8%D7%95%D7%AA-%D7%94%D7%A7%D7%A8%D7%A2-%D7%91%D7%99%D7%9F-%D7%93%D7%A8%D7%A2%D7%99.html (accessed January 1, 2014).

18. For a concise presentation of his message, see, for example, the booklet published by the Am Shalem party in the form of a newspaper: "BeLev Shalem – Hadevarim Laashuram," January 2013.

19. Asaf Sharabi and Shlomo Guzmen-Carmeli, "The Teshuva Bargain: Ritual Healing Performances at Rabbi Amnon Yitzchak's Rallies," *Journal of Ritual Studies* 27, no. 2 (2013): 97–110.

20. As part of the effort to humiliate Amnon Yitzhak, Shas insisted that the title 'rabbi' be omitted from the voting slips for his party, even though his followers universally

refer to him with this honorary title. Shas justified this demand by explaining that Amnon Yitzhak does not carry official certification as a rabbi.

21. Ilan Lior, "The Party that Wants to Restore the Power to the People," *Haaretz*, January 17, 2013.

22. David Lehmann and Batia Siebzehner, *Remaking Israeli Judaism: The Challenge of Shas* (London: Hurst, 2006).

23. Nissim Leon, "The Political Use of the Teshuva Cassette Culture in Israel," *Contemporary Jewry* 31, no. 2 (2011): 91–106.

24. "Amnon vs. Amnon", *Channel 10*, January 2, 2013.

25. Street poster: "Call to the Faithful by the Kabbalist Rabbi David Abuhatzeira."

26. Menachem Friedman, *Haredi [Ultra-orthodox] Society* [in Hebrew] (Jerusalem: Jerusalem Institute for Israel Studies, 1991), 70–88.

27. See, for example, Benjamin Brown, "Doktrinat Da'at Torah: Shlosha Shlavim," *Derekh haRuah* 2 (2005): 537–600; Martin Tessler, "Emdat Poskei Hahalakha Klapei Ma'arekhet Hamishpat shel Medinat Yisrael" (diss., Ben Gurion University of the Negev, 2009). For a critical view of this position, see Aharon Rose, "HaHaredim: Ketav Hagana," *Tekhelet* 25 (2008): 34–61.

28. See, for example, Nissim Leon, "Visions of Identity: Pictures of Rabbis in Haredi (Ultra-Orthodox) Private Homes in Israel," *Journal of Israeli History: Politics, Society, Culture* 32, no. 1 (2013): 87–108.

29. Street poster: "Rabbi Ovadia Weeps and You Sleep On?"

30. Data from the 18th Knesset Elections Committee and the 19th Knesset Elections Committee.

31. See, for example, Yohai Hakak, "Young Men in Israeli Haredi Yeshiva Education: the Scholars Enclave in Unrest," in *Jewish Identities in a Changing World*, ed. Eliezer Ben-Rafael, Yosef Gorny, and Judit Bokser Liwerant (Leiden: Brill, 2012); Nurit Stadler, "Playing with Sacred/Corporeal Identities: Yeshivah Students' Fantasies of Military Participation," *Jewish Social Studies* 13, no. 2 (2007): 155–78.

The political transformation of the Israeli 'Russian' street in the 2013 elections

Vladimir (Ze'ev) Khanin[a,b]

[a]Department of Middle Eastern Studies and Political Science, Ariel University;
[b]Department of Political Studies, Bar-Ilan University, Israel

The Great Aliya from the USSR and the post-Soviet states began a quarter of a century ago, bringing to Israel about 1.1 million Russian-speaking Jews and their family members. This population corresponds to approximately 19 Knesset seats, and is thus a crucial factor in Israeli electoral politics. From the late 1990s this community was almost equally divided in its sympathy between nationwide mainstream parties and Russian sectarian immigrant parties. However, if previously there were either purely sectarian or nationwide parties, in the past decade the majority of Russian Israelis prefer new types of political representation: either a 'Russian party with an Israeli accent' (mainly Israel Beiteinu) or an all-Israeli party with some Russian accent (i.e. Likud). Nevertheless, despite the similarities in the ideological orientations and socioeconomic views, the Russian-speaking supporters of both political parties represent two distinct political cultures among the Israeli community of former Soviet Union *olim* and their children. This may explain why the joint list of Likud–Israel Beiteinu during the 2013 Knesset elections experienced substantial losses of each party's traditional 'Russian' (as well as general) voters, many of whom opted this time for parties of the 'contentious middle class' – the right-wing Habayit Hayehudi and 'centrist' Yesh Atid. This article argues that in the coming years, the Russian community's politics in Israel will continue to search for an optimal model of combination of a party's ethnic base with a mainstream platform, and which constitute an exemplary model and inspiration of political participation for other ethnic or cultural identity oriented groups, such as English-, French- and Amharic-speaking immigrants, and for the 'new *haredim*'.

According to a popular stereotype in the media and some academic circles, the Russian Israelis have enjoyed the status of so-called 'king-makers' during the past 20 years. The unstable political preferences of the Russian-speaking immigrants, as well as their inconsistent partisan sympathies, brought about recurrent changes in the balance of forces within the Israeli political system. It is clear today that this stigma, as well as the idea that every ballot cast by former Soviet Union (FSU) immigrants constitutes a protest vote against the government, regardless of the identity of the ruling party, is based on the impression that the civic and political culture of Russian Israelis is dominated by the Soviet legacy. We believe this concept to be outdated.[1] However, there is no doubt that over the past two decades, the voting behaviour of this segment of voters has been crucial for the electoral success of the majority of Israeli Zionist parties, as well as for the potential of these parties' leaders to occupy key positions in the government.[2]

Today, the demographic impact of the Russian-speaking immigrant community remains highly important. According to a 1 January 2013 census, Israel was home to 862,419 persons of 18 years and over who had immigrated to the country from the USSR and post-Soviet states since the beginning of the so-called 'Great Aliya' in September 1989.[3] More than 24,500 descendants of the Russian-speaking *olim* of the 1990s have reached the voting age. These native-born Russian Israelis, together with Russian Jewish immigrants who arrived in Israel at the age of two years or younger, experienced their entire cultural and political socialization process in Israel. They represent the electoral constituency equivalent of one or one-and-a-half Knesset seats. All in all, in the 2013 elections, members of Russian-Israeli families were about 16% of the 5.6 million Israeli citizens of voting age.

The electoral potential of the Russian-Israeli Jewish community thus corresponded to approximately 19 Knesset seats. The 66–70% voting participation of this group is normally higher than the 62–65% average of the general population. Since the 1999 elections, the higher level of political participation increased the actual political influence of the Israeli 'Russian' community, and could have increased their electoral potential representation to 20–21 parliamentary seats. However, in the 2003 elections, the Russian-Israeli street demonstrated a lower level of electoral participation. Less than 60% of the Israeli Russians voted, whereas the electoral participation in the general population reached 67.7%.[4] As a result, the Russian street lost 1–2 Knesset seats of its 19-seat potential.[5]

It was the Israel Beiteinu (Israel – Our Home) party, founded by Avigdor Lieberman in 1999, which has become the strongest political force of Russian Israelis over the past decade. This party initially presented itself not only as the political wing of the FSU immigrant community, but also – and over time, even predominantly – as an all-Israeli pragmatic right-wing movement. Furthermore, in the recent elections, Israel Beiteinu ran alongside the ruling party, Likud, in a Likud–Israel Beiteinu coalition. Another political party, the purely Russian immigrant sectarian party Israelim (Israelis), attempted to repeat the spirit and success of the former Israel b'Aliya party, led by Natan Sharansky.[6] Israel b'Aliya had enjoyed an unpredictable success in the 1996 elections (seven Knesset seats) and was, for several years to follow, the major political expression of the Israeli Russian-speaking community. The contemporary Israelim party, however, did not pass the electoral threshold.

The 2013 elections raised some important questions regarding the Russian-Israeli community and its political culture. We are witnessing the conclusion of the social process of Israelization of the political bodies affiliated with the Russian street. If that is so, then why did the 2011 social protests, which influenced the elections, have no impact on the Russian voter? To what extent does the Israelization trend in Russian politics reflect the social and civic integration process of FSU immigrants within Israeli society? And, can the Russian-Jewish political expression in Israel, in its current form, serve as an efficient model for other socio-cultural groups in Israel, such as immigrants from English-speaking countries, from France and, especially, from Ethiopia?

The Russian-Jewish community in Israel: a political structure and voting trends

The model of electoral behaviour of Israelis from the FSU had stabilized by the second half of the 1990s. Since then, the community has been almost equally divided in its partisan sympathy between general nationwide parties and Russian immigrant sectarian parties. The community is further divided between those who give priority to issues related to foreign policy, security and Israeli national identity, and those whose political decisions are governed by domestic social and economic considerations, such as housing, employment, welfare or civil rights.

The more the community's wellbeing increased, the more the political weight of the first group gradually increased. According to a recent survey, 54–57% of FSU immigrants reported that they were mainly concerned with security issues and foreign affairs, and expressed interest in mainstream rather than sectarian politics platforms.[7] An opinion poll conducted during the 2013 electoral campaign showed that political parties which stressed a social and economic agenda were likely to raise sympathy from the remaining 35–44% Russians who had previously preferred other political options.[8] While the first group (voters more concerned with security and foreign affairs) is better represented among the electorate of mainstream Israeli parties, the second group (voters more concerned with social and economic issues) tends to vote for sectarian or identity-oriented parties. Both Leshem and Khanin's study of 2011[9] and the 2013 Shvakim Panorama, an opinion poll for Russian-speaking Israelis,[10] found that the less the immigrants were interested in Russian language and culture, the less they intended to vote for parties with an agenda that focused on their community's interests.

Between 1996 and 2003, there were either purely sectarian or national parties. In the recent decade, however, supporters of these two types of political parties have expressed their interest in a new model of political organization. The abovementioned survey found that at least two-thirds of Russian Israelis sympathized with a 'Russian party with an Israeli accent' or an 'all-Israeli party with some Russian accent'. Since 2003, Lieberman's Israel Beitenu party has dominated within the first group, while Likud dominated the second. Between 2006 and 2009 the Russian Israelis who preferred an all-Israeli party were divided between the Likud and Kadima parties. It appears that, contrary to the media stereotype, the majority of the FSU immigrants supported moderate, mainly centre-right parties, and to a lesser extent centre and centre-left parties, and were less likely to support the extreme-right parties.[11]

The potential of purely Russian immigrant lists usually does not exceed one or one-and-a-half Knesset seats. In practice, they do not get more than 1% of the total Russian vote. National party lists without any Russian accent get two or three parliamentary seats from the Russian constituency. This trend was found as early as 2004,[12] a year after the disappointing results of the 2003 Knesset elections, which dramatically decreased parliamentary representation of Russian Israelis. It was reflected yet again in March and April 2009, soon after the 18th Knesset elections.[13] According to the abovementioned studies, the share of those who supported the idea of a Russian party decreased from approximately 50% in 2004 to one-third in 2009, while the concept of a clear-cut sectarian Russian immigrant party was supported by just 5% of the respondents. The majority of this group, more than a quarter of the entire sample, supported the concept of a Russian immigrant party with a mainstream agenda.

On the other hand, while the supporters of the idea of a mainstream party with a strong Russian wing showed moderate growth from a third of the community's voters in 2004 up to some 40% in 2009, the percentage of FSU immigrants believing that the Russian community has no need for any special political representation doubled from 12% to 25%. Research that was done two years later showed that this spectrum was almost entirely unchanged, as indicated in Table 1.

In this case, the preference that was given by the immigrant voters to a certain model of a political movement – the Russian sectarian, the nationwide with a Russian accent, and the mainstream (without any accented immigrant connotation) – does not necessarily mean their affiliation with distinctly different political parties. In the 2006 and 2009 elections, for example, Israel Beiteinu, which positioned itself as a nationwide political party whose voters, for historical reasons, speak mostly Russian, obtained about one-half of the entire Russian-Israeli vote, which corresponded to 19 or 20 Knesset mandates. Studies showed that at least four of these approximately 10 Russian seats came from those who voted for Israel Beiteinu as the only legitimate Russian party – whether with an Israeli accent or not. Another four seats were given to Israel

Table 1. Which political parties are preferable for Russian-speaking Israelis (%)?

Party models	Census			
	2004	March 2009	May 2009	2011
Russian immigrant party	51	30	30	31
A nationwide party with a strong immigrant wing	33	41	37	44
No need for any special political representation	12	25	28	25
Do not know/not sure	4	4	5	–
Total	100	100	100	100

Beiteinu by those who supported it as a nationwide party with a Russian accent. Finally, it gained support among those FSU immigrants who supported Israel Beiteinu's platform and its charismatic leader without any specific ethnic or community concern.

The Likud electorate, which in 2006–2009 was shared with Kadima, and since has dominated in the niche of Israeli parties with a Russian accent, also had two categories of Russian-speaking voters. One category included those who believed that the Likud was on the way to establish a strong Russian branch, led by Yuli Edelstein and Ze'ev Elkin, and the other included those whose political priorities were beyond the ethnic community margins.

At the same time, there is a substantial – approximately equivalent to five or six Knesset seats – potential for votes which are floating on the borderline between all-nation and sectarian segments of the Russian-Israeli community politics. The majority of this group of mostly moderate, right-wing, and social and civic issues-oriented Russian-speaking voters in 1999 predominantly supported the Russian centrist Israel b'Aliya party. In 2003, many of them voted for the anti-ultra-Orthodox Shinui party; in 2006 they then divided their support between social-liberal Kadima and the social wing of Israel Beiteinu; and in 2009, in various percentages, they voted for Israel Beiteinu, Likud and Kadima. At some point, former Israel b'Aliya voters in this group were joined by Russian Sharonists – personal devotees of Ariel Sharon, who after the 2005 split of the Likud followed him to the new Kadima party. Yet after the 2006 elections many of them left this party, and in 2009 shared their ballots between Likud and Israel Beiteinu.

The strengthening of this camp in 2009 occurred mostly due to the fact that Lieberman had openly challenged the existing rules of the Israeli political game, established in the 1990s. These rules meant that all de facto Israeli elites agreed that sectarian leaders have a right to an almost monopolistic control of their natural voters. In return for this concession, the sectarian parties are expected not to aspire to have more than the status of a junior partner. They also should not interfere in the sphere of nationwide interests.

Breaking this unwritten convention by addressing both the Hebrew- and Russian-speaking electorate of nationwide parties, Lieberman simultaneously opened the sphere of Israel Beiteinu's natural domination. That meant that part of the Russian-Jewish community, which normally prefers to support Russian sectarian lists, became a legitimate target for those mainstream parties that were willing to open their infrastructure to the establishment of strong immigrant wings and to demonstrate a Russian accent in their activities. They thus succeeded in attracting part of the floating Russian vote.[14]

Unsurprisingly, these floating voters are normally among the first who, together with the extended Russian-speaking electorate of the mainstream Israeli parties, come back to sit on the fence straight after the elections, as the need for an immediate political choice disappears. That happened after the 2009 elections: two independent opinion polls[15] conducted in late October and early November

2010 showed that the leaders of Israel Beiteinu, Likud and Kadima lost most of their floating Russian vote, but kept their traditional strong Russian electoral core. According to these polls, if elections had taken place then, Israel Beiteinu would have got 8–9 seats (out of the 10 or 11 Russian seats obtained in 2009); Likud would still have controlled 3–3.5 of 4.5–5 seats, and Kadima would have got 1.5 of the approximately 2.5 Russian seats obtained by these parties in 2009. Our conservative estimate was that the potential of the actively undecided (i.e. those who did not know whom they would vote for, but would most probably participate in the next elections) was equivalent to the same 4–6 seats, floating between the all-nation and sectarian parties.

As far as the other parties were concerned, their potential showing on the Russian street was, as in the past, much more modest – from a half to almost one seat to Shas (mostly among immigrants from the Oriental republics of the former Soviet Union); between 0.3 to 0.5 of a Knesset seat to Labour; and about two seats for the remainder of the mainstream left-wing and right-wing together.[16]

This means that in the middle of the previous Knesset period, there were still no radical changes among the Russian-Israeli electorate. One might have expected that the same three parties – Israel Beiteinu, Likud and Kadima – would continue to dominate among their strong Russian core, as well as among the undecided Russian-speaking voters. Obviously, they would have no other options but to choose either the only Russian party with a nationwide agenda (Israel Beiteinu) or one of the Israeli parties with a Russian accent (Likud or Kadima).

This did not happen, however. By early 2013, Russian-speaking Israelis presented a substantially different political configuration, which changed dramatically about six months before the elections. This occurred because of two events: the formation of the Likud–Israel Beiteinu joint list, and the change in Kadima's leadership and the political 'zigzagging' of its new chairman, Shaul Mofaz.

The Russian street and 19th Knesset election results

To obtain a comprehensive picture of the Russian-Israeli voting for the 19th Knesset, we used four different sources of information. First, we used the official voting results of the 60 polling stations which were opened in the areas where Russian-speakers composed 85% of the population or more. Second, we made use of the results from the internal, non-public polls of the Russian-speaking immigrants ordered by different political parties. Third, we used the results of the public, nationwide electoral polls conducted the day before, the very day, and the day after the elections. Finally, we made use of the results of exit polls of the Russian-speaking Israelis conducted on election day in 11 polling stations within nine cities – Jerusalem, Modiin, Beit-Shemesh and Ariel in the centre of the country, Haifa, Karmiel and Katsrin in the north, and Beer-Sheva in the south.[17] According to these sources, the Russian vote was distributed as indicated in Table 2.

Table 2. Russian immigrants' voting trends in the 2009 and 2013 Knesset elections

2009 elections

Parties	% at Russian polling stations	Opp. poll, Feb. 2009	Seats
Israel Beiteinu	56.8	57.5	10–11
Likud	21.5	23.4	4.5–5
Kadima	13	13.8	2.5
Mafdal	0.4	0.5	0.25
Ihud Leumi	0.8		
Avoda	2.1	1.7	0.4
Merets	0.5	0.3	0.1
Shas	2.9	1.1	0.6
Yahadut Ha-Tora	0.5	0.1	0.1
Aliya	0.4	0.1	0.1
Lev, Leeder	0.2	0.1	
Yarukim, Ale-Jarok	0.8	0.4	0.2
Other	1.4	1	0.25
Total	100	100	20
Estimated voting cast %		67	

2013 elections

Parties	% at Russian polling stations	Exit poll, 22 Feb. 2013	Seats
Likud-Beiteinu	56.0	61	10–10.5
Kadima	1.0	1	
Yesh Atid	11.0	12	3
Ha-Tnua	4.3	3.5	
Jewish Home (Mafdal-IL)	5.7	5	1.2
Strong Israel	1.1	1	
Avoda	4.9	4	0.8
Merets	1.4	1	0.25
Shas	4.2	1.5	0.8
Yahadut Ha-Tora	0.7	0.5	0.1
Israelis	4.3	4	0.8
Economy, Leeder	0.4	–	
Yarukim, Ale-Jarok	2.6	5.5	0.5
Other	2.9		0.3
Total	100	58	17–18

One can conclude from this data that the most dramatic changes took place in the centre-left section of the Russian-Israeli community's political spectrum. This was the case among former voters of the initially centrist, and then moderately left-wing Kadima, which in 2006–2009 headed the government and in 2009–2013 was the leading opposition party. It had the biggest parliamentary faction in the 18th Knesset, including 2–2.5 seats obtained by this party among Russian-speakers. A gradual but continuous decrease in the support for this party started immediately after the 2009 Knesset elections, due to the unsuccessful political manoeuvrings of its newly elected leader, Shaul Mofaz. Kadima joined and then subsequently abandoned the Netanyahu-led government. It also sent contradictory messages with regard to core issues in the Israeli political debate, such as the peace process, the Hamas regime in Gaza, the nuclear threat of Iran, Jewish ultra-Orthodox and Israeli Palestinians' military service, etc.

In the 2013 elections, Kadima recruited barely sufficient support to pass the electoral threshold. Its Russian electorate had almost totally disappeared by election day. Most of these voters shifted to Kadima's successor centre-left parties: Ha-Tnua ('The Movement'), founded by former Kadima leader Tzipi Livni and, to a larger extent, to Yesh Atid ('There is a Future'), led by Yair Lapid.

Changes in the centre-right and the right were less dramatic but still substantial. Some 60% of the Russian vote went to the joint list of Likud–Israel Beitenu. This corresponds to 10 or 11 Knesset seats, which is 4–5 seats fewer than both parties held together in the previous Knesset (10–11 – Israel Beiteinu; 4.5–5 – Likud). Indeed, opinion polls after the establishment of the Israel Beiteinu–Likud alliance showed that almost a quarter of their former voters did not intend to support the new political alliance between the two parties. Most of these drop-out former Israel Beiteinu and Likud supporters did not move their support to other parties, but rather moved to the 'undecided' category,[18] where they remained until the elections. As polls showed, the differences between Likud–Israel Beiteinu and other parties were perceived as rather substantial.[19]

At the same time, Likud and Israel Beiteinu did not suffer equal electoral losses. According to a poll, some 60% of the Russian immigrants who previously voted for Israel Beiteinu were ready to do so again in 2013, while 35% more were sitting on the fence. Among former Russian Likud voters the situation was exactly the opposite.[20] It can be concluded that Israel Beiteinu preserved most of its Russian electorate, as well as a substantial part of its all-Israeli electorate, which the party was able to mobilize into the joint list with Likud. Most of the losses – 11 out of 42 Knesset seats previously occupied by the two parties in 2009 – were actually lost by Likud.

In previous Knesset elections, the share of middle-class, middle-aged Russian-speakers among the electorate of Likud was higher than among the electorate of Israel Beiteinu. At that time it attracted a disproportionally high number of underprivileged young and older Russian-speaking immigrants.[21] Many former Likud voters thus shifted their support to parties which promised to represent and defend the interests of the middle class – i.e. the religious Zionist party Habayit Hayehudi ('Jewish Home'), led by Naftali Bennett, and the new middle-class party Yesh Atid, led by Yair Lapid.

A Shvakim Panorama opinion poll showed that about 50% of Russian-speaking immigrants who voted for Yesh Atid and 21% of those who voted for Habayit Hayehudi mentioned Likud–Israel Beiteinu as their second option. This means that in the right-wing camp Likud–Israel Beiteinu and Yesh Atid together with Habayit HaYehudi competed, to a certain extent, for the same constituency of the Russian-speaking, most of them former Likud voters. Among potential Likud–Beiteinu Russian-speaking immigrant voters there were many who believed that national security is more important than a strong economy, while potential supporters of Yesh Atid and Habayit Hayehudi believed otherwise.[22]

Generally speaking, of the 17–18 Russian seats that were jointly obtained in 2009 by the Russian non-sectarian Israel Beiteinu (10–11) and the two mainstream parties with a Russian accent – Likud (4.5–5) and Kadima (2–2.5) – one or two seats were lost in 2013 due to the decrease in electoral participation of Russian-speaking Israelis. Of the remainder, some 10 seats were obtained by Likud–Israel Beiteinu; approximately three went to Kadima successors – Yesh Atid and HaTnua ('The Movement') led by Tzipi Livni; about one seat went to Habayit Hayehudi; and less than one seat to other parties.

Most importantly, among the latter was the purely Russian sectarian party Israelim ('Israelis') of David Kon, which in addition to a few hundred votes inherited from its immediate predecessor, the sectarian Israel Mitkhadeshet party ('Renewed Israel'), in 2009 also succeeded in obtaining about a half of a Russian mandate from Israel Beiteinu.[23] About half of the potential Israelim voters declared in the abovementioned Shvakim Panorama poll that the Likud–Israel Beiteinu list was their second possible option.

A few hundred votes were again obtained by the Progressive Liberal Democratic Party, Leader. It positioned itself as a party of 'ethnic Russians in Israel'. So, two 'narrowly sectarian Russian' parties, which did not even come close to the 2% electoral threshold, together received a number of votes corresponding to about one Knesset seat. As noted above, this corresponds to the existing potential of a purely sectarian Russian immigrant party.

The 2013 Knesset elections brought no surprises to the Russian street. According to our data, political parties which did not put any specific emphasis on Russian-Jewish interests in their electoral platforms, or were unable to do so effectively, jointly scored no more than two or three Russian seats. These votes, in different proportions went, on the one hand, to the left-wing Avoda (Labour) and radical-left Meretz, and on the other hand to the most right-wing party, Ozma Le-Israel ('Strength of Israel'). Others who benefited from Russian votes were non-Russian sectarian and ultra-religious parties – Sephardic Shas (which usually gets between 0.3 and 0.5 of at seat from people originating in Oriental FSU republics) and the Yahadut Ha-Torah ('Torah Judaism') bloc. There were various social protest movements, such as the ecologist parties, in particular Ale Yarok ('Green Leaf'), which attracted many hundreds of young

Russian-speakers, among other liberal-oriented voters and those disappointed in the Israeli political system.

Netanyahu's interest, Lieberman's dilemma and the Russian-Israeli street

One might say that Likud and Israel Beiteinu are both winners of the elections, while at the same time they are the main losers in the Russian street, and so far as the general public is concerned. Shortly before the political alliance, the leader of neither party excluded this scenario.[24] So why then did Netanyahu, and especially Lieberman, take the risk of losing many Knesset seats if, after the elections, both parties most probably would have joined forces anyhow and formed a coalition?

Netanyahu's main interest was not only to become the leader of the biggest Knesset faction, but to defeat his rivals by a large margin. The political alliance with Israel Beiteinu was designed to meet this challenge in spite of the expected loss of seats. This had been predicted by some of the polls at the beginning of the election campaign.[25] The union would make Netanyahu the uncontested candidate for the position of Prime Minister, as well as the leader of the faction which would clearly dominate the future coalition government. As for Lieberman, his decision to join the electoral bloc was well thought through. According to him, the negotiations for merging the parties started at least a year before the elections. For a short while, the negotiations were interrupted, when Kadima joined Netanyahu's coalition in 2012, but in general, Lieberman and his inner circle's efforts to bring about a political alliance with Likud were motivated by personal-strategic reasons.[26]

Lieberman has never hidden his political ambitions. He wants one day to become Israel's Prime Minister. This possibility, at least in the last five years, has held some credibility in Israeli public discourse. Beginning in 2006 or 2007, Israeli pollsters monitoring the public popularity of various candidates for the prime ministerial position started to include Lieberman's name. Some observers believe that Israel may have a Russian Prime Minister within the next few Knesset election periods.[27]

Lieberman would be able to achieve this goal as a legitimate leader of a dominant Israeli political movement, preferably a right-leaning or National Camp movement. Since the beginning of his political activity, Lieberman has been linked to the Likud. By the late 1980s, he had become a key member of Netanyahu's political circle. The latter played a crucial role in his rise to power in the party, when Netanyahu appointed Lieberman as director-general of Likud in 1993. After Netanyahu's victory in the 1996 elections, Lieberman became the Director-General of the Prime Minister's Office. The growing power of Lieberman within the Likud attracted internal opposition and upset internal rivals during the mid-1990s. Not receiving any substantial support from Netanyahu, Lieberman left the Likud in 1997, accompanied by many Russian Likud activists as well as by Israeli-born supporters, some of whom were very disappointed with Netanyahu's readiness to accept the Oslo Accords with the PLO. These groups of activists, together with secessionist right-wing members of the Russian sectarian-centrist Israel b'Aliya party, and a few of the Russian municipal lists, formed the initial structure of Lieberman's new party, Israel Beiteinu, which won two seats in the 1999 Knesset elections.

More than 90%, more than 80% and some 70% of the Israel Beiteinu vote, in the 1999, 2006 and 2009 Knesset elections respectively, came from Russian-speakers. Yet it was clear that Lieberman had no intention of creating another Russian sectarian movement. He initially positioned Israel Beiteinu as a mainstream right-wing party, in which most representatives are of Russian origins. In order to stress the national position of his party, Lieberman allied with the right-wing National Unity bloc, but this alliance proved to be unsuccessful in the 2003 elections. As from 2004, Israel Beiteinu operated as an independent political force, aiming at providing a mainstream political alternative to the Likud, loyal to revisionist ideology and eager to lead the Israeli national camp.

This ambitious goal was largely perceived as a far-flung fantasy until the 2006 elections, in which Israel Beiteinu gained 11 Knesset seats, only one seat less than Likud. Over time, the share of Israeli-born and non-Russian speakers among Israel Beiteinu's supporters grew. In 2009, these groups brought the party about five of its total 15 seats. As far as the Russian-Israeli street is concerned, as we mentioned elsewhere,[28] Israel Beiteinu succeeded in solving the problem of finding a *modus vivendi* between its nationwide aspirations and the predominantly Russian character of its electoral base. Israel Beiteinu's agenda became attractive for a growing number of immigrants seeking access to the national decision-making process, without being identified with an identity-oriented ethnic party.

The success of Israel Beiteinu in the 2009 elections was, however, only partial. Targeting the higher position of the Israeli political leadership required yet a broader layer of national legitimacy. In search of modalities to 'upgrade' Israel Beiteinu, Lieberman considered the alliance with Likud as a constructive step towards national leadership. For Lieberman, being 'number 2' in the Likud–Israel Beiteinu list meant bringing Israel Beiteinu closer to a position of national leadership. He was now among the top candidates to inherit Netanyahu's leadership in the Israeli right-wing camp, leaving behind some of his old rivals within the former elite of Likud. With the formation of the Likud–Beiteinu list, Lieberman was convinced that he had greatly advanced toward his goal of becoming a leader of the Israeli right. However, the alliance presented new risks, as the union with the Likud could alienate the core supporters of Israel Beiteinu, who still seek political expression in a party which is for the most part affiliated with the Russian street.

Why Russian Jews (again) did not vote for the left

The number of Russian-speaking Israelis who supported genuine left-wing and centre-left parties[29] this time – as in the past – was minimal. Although the

Russian-Jewish electorate of Avoda and Meretz together doubled from 2–2.5% in 2009 to 5–6% in 2013 (about 0.5 and almost one seat, respectively), this can hardly be regarded as a break-through of the left-wing parties on the Russian street. This trend might seem strange, at first glance, since the overwhelming majority of FSU immigrants have been living in Israel for more than 20 years. Moreover, there are some 200,000 Israelis who were born into Russian-speaking families. Many believe that the current social conditions can facilitate the full integration of the Russian-speaking Israelis into the political system, and they should therefore be proportionally represented on both sides of the Israeli political cleavage. Recent sociological studies suggest that the major models of behaviour of Russian-speaking immigrants, including those related to political culture, are influenced by their Israeli experience, rather than their Russian origins or the Soviet legacy.[30]

Observers usually mention two basic reasons for this phenomenon. The majority of the Russian-speaking Jews in Israel are socially market-oriented. They share a moderate right-wing ideology and are thus a natural electorate for relevant parties, like the centre-right Likud and Israel Beiteinu. These have both a liberal market ideology and a strong social outlook. In addition, in the conscience of the average Russian-speaking immigrant, the social and economic programme of the Israeli left is strongly coupled with the call for territorial and ideological concessions to the Palestinians and the Arab world. Therefore the social phraseology of the left-wing parties is less than attractive for FSU immigrants, especially if one considers that a similar phraseology exists in elements of the national camp.

Theoretically, this state of affairs might have changed due to the huge wave of social protest movements which took place in Israel in the summer of 2011, against the increasing housing prices and the general cost of living. Contrary to previous economically oriented protests in Israel, the events of 2011 expressed the distress of middle class, rather than focusing on the welfare needs of the working poor or of the underclass. The protesters claimed that they are the main source of the nation's economic strength and of carrying most of the military security burden, and they do not get enough in return.[31]

Leaders of Israeli left-wing parties, who shaped their campaign in the spirit of these protests, identified the FSU immigrants with the protesting middle class, and thus expected that this time they would be able to recruit political support among Russian voters. This political opportunity was further emphasized when the Labour party leader, Shelly Yachimovich, almost completely ignored or silenced the Palestinian issue and the peace process in the electoral campaign and only championed, for the most part, the messages of the social protest. However, the relative failure of this tactic had more to do with the nature of the social protest itself, rather than with the messages of the left-wing parties' campaigns. The Russian presence among the summer 2011 protesters and campaigners was relatively small. As a community, Russian-speaking Israelis did not show much enthusiasm towards the movement. Most of them identified the protest with the young generation of the established Israeli elite or powerful elements within Israeli society, or, as sociologist Baruch Kimmerling coined it, the 'Ahusalim'[32] (an acronym of the Hebrew words for Ashkenazi, secular, socialist and national). In the Russian street, the protest was rather perceived as a campaign carried out by the Ahusalim in order to preserve the privileged status and interests of the stronger, and rather hegemonic, elements of Israeli society, following the economic liberalization and the growing competition in the fields of culture, education and the economy. In sharp contrast to the Israeli media representation of the protest, which framed the movement as a collective cry for social justice and solidarity, FSU immigrants viewed the protest as a corporative struggle of the 'First Israel' against the growing power of the 'Third Israel'. When the social protests voiced social demands related to housing prices and cost of living, the Russian street could not avoid recalling the economic and social difficulties the FSU immigrants had experienced themselves not so long ago.[33] As Leonid Lutsky, editor-in-chief of the popular Russian-Israeli newspaper *Globus*, explained:

> The younger generation of the 'First Israel' found itself in a difficult and uncomfortable socio-economic situation, and protested against it. However, it was the same situation that new immigrants from the FSU experienced 15–29 years ago. At that time these veteran elite groups considered these difficulties as ordinary and acceptable. So why should the immigrants support them now?[34]

Moreover, the FSU immigrants felt alienated from the centre of the protest, and especially from the iconic 'Tent City' on the prestigious and trendy Rothschild Boulevard. The movement leaders' efforts to redirect the spontaneous mass protest against imbalances in the free market toward more socialist or anti-liberal ideologies, and the pseudo-radical ornaments used by the protesters, such as red flags, posters with portraits of Che Guevara or Mao Zedong, and slogans such as 'Marx Was Right', alarmed the Russian immigrants, and pushed them away from the Israeli left.

Conclusion

The results of the 2013 Knesset elections proved, once again, the dominant trend in the political world-view of Russian-speaking Israelis in the last decade: 70–89% of Russian voters are interested in neither sectarian Russian nor purely nationwide parties. They prefer a 'Russian party with an Israeli accent', or an all-Israeli party with a strong Russian-speaking branch. Israel Beiteinu and the Likud respectively remained the only relevant options for voters with such preferences. Studies conducted during the 18th Knesset electoral campaign showed that Israel Beiteinu and Likud were competing for more or less the same groups of Russian- and Hebrew-speaking centre-right potential voters. This was one of the major considerations in the formation of the political alliance between Israel Beiteinu and Likud.

However, in spite of the similarities in the ideological orientations and the socio-economic views of Russian-speaking supporters of both political parties, Likud and Israel Beiteinu still reflect distinct and different political cultures, and mark the specificity of the FSU *olim* and of their native-born children as voters. These two categories of voters, as one may conclude from the election results, would prefer 'their' parties to promote their political agendas and cooperate in the government *after* the elections, rather than forming long- or short-term alliances. The leaders of Israel Beiteinu and Likud may have realized this preference, as their parties ran for the 2013 municipal elections on separate lists. They also decided to split the Knesset joint list several months after the elections.

These attitudes have a substantial impact on the ideology and strategy of the Russian-Israeli political elites. These groups are likely to continue to be divided into two major camps. The first, the Lieberman camp, promotes the model of integration into the local establishment from a position of strength and through the implementation of the Russian-Jewish neo-Zionist values into Israeli political discourse.[35] The second camp, the Likud-based Sharansky and Edelstein camp, follows the concept of 'influence from within', promoting the Russian community's interests by cooperation and exchange of resources with influential intra- and inter-party clans of the old elite.

It is also very likely that the third, sectarian camp of the Russian-speaking politicians will remain marginal due the narrow niche that remains for purely Russian sectarian parties. This was shown by the electoral failure of the Israelim list. These parties may, at best, together score one or one-and-a-half Knesset seats.

The dominance of Israel Beiteinu and Likud in the Russian street does not imply, however, that Russian-speaking Israelis, especially the younger generations, are entirely and automatically 'in the pocket' of moderate right-wing social market-oriented parties. The share of young voters and of the young families who supported middle-class parties – the right-wing Habayit Hayehudi and the centrist Yesh Atid – was higher than these age groups' percentage of the population in general.

Future developments of Russian community politics in Israel in the coming years – and maybe even decades – will take place in the context of 'multiculturalism within the Jewish collective', adopted by Israeli society since early 1980s. That means that there will be a constant search for an optimal model of combining a party's ethnic base with a mainstream platform and meeting the demand for general and social legitimization of sectarian-mainstream interests.

One cannot exclude the possibility that this model may also be attractive for new sectarian elites who are now entering the Israeli political market. The first in line are immigrants from Ethiopia, who at least three times – in 2006, 2009 and 2013 – tried, in vain, to have their representatives elected to the Knesset on a separate party ticket. English-speaking immigrants, who in 2003 first tried to present themselves as an independent political force under the umbrella of Nathan Sharansky's Russian Israel b'Aliya party,[36] as well as the so-called 'new haredim'[37] and especially the immigrants from Francophone countries, might be the next three prospective political groups to attempt to follow this model,

The Russian immigrants' political behaviour and participation constitute a distinct political model which might remain in the Israeli political landscape in the near and, quite likely, more distant future.

Notes on contributor

Vladimir (Ze'ev) Khanin is an Associate Professor in the Department of Political, Israeli and Middle Eastern Studies at Ariel University, and lectures in Political Science at Bar-Ilan University. He is also Chief Scientist of the Israeli Ministry for Alia and Immigrant Absorption.

Disclosure statement

No potential conflict of interest was reported by the author.

Notes

1. Vladimir (Ze'ev) Khanin, "Russian-Jewish Political Experience in Israel: Patterns, Elites and Movements," *Israel Affairs* 17, no. 1 (2011): 56–72.
2. Vladimir (Ze'ev) Khanin, "Israel's 'Russian' Parties," in *Contemporary Israel: Domestic Politics, Foreign Policy, and Security Challenges*, ed. Robert O. Freedman (Boulder, Colorado: Westview Press, 2008), 97–114; Vladimir (Ze'ev) Khanin, *The "Russians" and Power in the State of Israel: Establishment of the USSR/CIS Immigrant Community and its Impact on the Political Structure of the Country* [in Russian] (Moscow: Institute for Israel and Middle Eastern Studies, 2004), 18–38; See also Zvi Gitelman and Ken Goldstein, "The 'Russian Revolution' in Israeli Politics" [in Hebrew], in *The 1999 Elections in Israel*, ed. Asher Arian and Michal Shamir (Jerusalem: Israeli Democracy Institute, 2001), 203–29.
3. The statistical data used in this paper comes from the Israeli Ministry of Aliya and Immigrant Absorption, unless otherwise stated. I wish to express my sincere thanks to Sigal Leybowich, director, and Shalom Ben-Yishaya and Dr Ruth Paley, chief officials, MOIA Department of information systems for their valuable assistance with the data collection.
4. Alexander Kogan, "Nudelman: Repatriates Saved Netanyahu Despite their Apathy," *Izrus*, January 25, 2013, http://izrus.co.il/obshina/article/2013-01-25/20337.html (accessed September 1, 2013).
5. Often neglected in political calculations, one should also consider the role of another section of the Russian street: the veterans of the Aliya of the 1970s. This group is conservatively estimated at 35–45,000 people, the equivalent of one Knesset seat and more. As previous studies show, the 1970 veterans identify with the FSU immigrant community and support its affiliated parties. However, due to statistical complications, the precise electoral potential of the 'veterans' is usually not accounted for. One should however consider this fact in defining the upper and bottom levels of statistical estimates of the total number of Russian-Israeli voters.
6. On Israel b'Aliya and other 'Russian' Israeli parties of the first generation, see Vladimir (Ze'ev) Khanin, "The New Russian Jewish Diaspora and 'Russian' Party Politics in Israel," *Nationalism and Ethnic Politics* 8, no. 4 (2002): 54–81.
7. Elazar Leshem and Vladimir (Ze'ev) Khanin, *Civil Identity of the FSU Immigrants of 1990–2010 in Israel. Research Report Submitted to the Israeli Ministry of Immigrant Absorption* (Ariel: Ariel University, 2012), 42.
8. Shvakim Panorama, *Report of FSU Immigrants' Public Opinion* [in Hebrew], December 17–24, 2012, 7.

9. Leshem and Khanin, *Civil Identity*.
10. Shvakim Panorama, *Report of FSU Immigrants' Public Opinion*, 8.
11. Khanin, "Israel's 'Russian' Parties."
12. Mutagim opinion poll, May 2004.
13. Mutagim opinion poll, March and April 2009.
14. Vladimir (Ze'ev) Khanin, "The Israel Beiteinu (Israel Our Home) Party between the Mainstream and "Russian" Community Politics," *Israel Affairs* 16, no. 1 (2010): 119.
15. Mutagim agency opinion poll, October 25, 2010; Geo-Cartography Agency opinion poll, November 2, 2010.
16. For details see Vladimir (Ze'ev) Khanin, "Distribution of Political Forces in the Israeli 'Russian Street' vis-à-vis Preconditions for the Government Coalition Crises" [in Russian], Position paper, Moscow Institute for Middle Eastern Studies, November 22, 2010, http://www.iimes.ru/?p=11721 (accessed September 1, 2013).
17. The study, designed by Sam Kliger, Director of the Research Institute for New Americans (RINA) and Vladimir (Ze'ev) Khanin, was implemented and funded by RINA and conducted on the day of the elections with the assistance of the ASK Data Collecting Agency, Israel.
18. Shvakim Panorama, *Report of FSU Immigrants' Public Opinion*, 10.
19. Ibid., 20–22.
20. Mutagim agency opinion poll, December 2012.
21. Mutagim agency opinion poll, March 2009. For more details see Vladimir (Ze'ev) Khanin, "Israeli Russian Voting Trends in the 2009 Knesset Elections," Position paper. Frederich Ebert Stiftung, August 2009.
22. Shvakim Panorama, *Report of FSU Immigrants' Public Opinion*, 11, 20
23. During the electoral campaign, the Israeli media discussed a possible 'conspiracy theory', which claimed that HaTnua founders Tzipi Livni and Haim Ramon supported the 'Russian' Party 'Israelim', with the goal of poaching votes from Yisrael Beiteinu. That, of course, was officially denied by both Livni and the Israelim party leaders. See Mati Tuchfeld, "Analysis: Who is Behind the New Immigrant Party 'The Israelis'?," *Israel Hayom*, December 18, 2013.
24. Personal interview with MK Avigdor Lieberman, Jerusalem, May 2013.
25. Lahav Harkov, "Right Loses 4 Seats from Likud–Beytenu Merger," *Jerusalem Post*, November 2, 2012; Gil Hoffman, "'Post' Poll Finds Olmert Unwanted in Politics," *Jerusalem Post*, November 15, 2012.
26. For a comprehensive discussion of the motives of the Israel Beiteinu leaders see Vladimir (Ze'ev) Khanin, "Why Lieberman Needs an Alliance with Netanyahu" [in Russian], *Moscow Institute for Middle Eastern Studies*, November 17, 2012.
27. See Eli Bardenstein, "Russian Prime Minister? It's Just a Question of Time," *Ma'ariv*, July 25, 2013.
28. Khanin, "The Israel Beiteinu," 112–17.
29. Not including Yesh Atid, which was perceived as the political endeavour of some left-wing elites, but clearly positioned itself as a centre party
30. For a review of scholarly literature on this issue see Khanin, "Russian-Jewish Political Experience"; Leshem and Khanin, "Civil Identity of the FSU Immigrants."
31. For a discussion, see Uri Ram and Dani Filk, "The 14th of July of Daphni Leef: The Rise and Fall of the Social Protest" [in Hebrew], *Theory and Criticism* 41 (2013): 17–43.
32. See Baruch Kimmerling, "State Building, State Autonomy and the Identity of Society – the Case of Israel," *Journal of Historical Sociology* 6, no. 4 (1993): 396–429; and Baruch Kimmerling, *The End of the Power of* Ahusalim [in Hebrew] (Jerusalem: Keter, 2005).

33. See Zvi Eckstein and Yoram Weiss, "On the Wage Growth of Immigrants: Israel, 1990–2000," IZA, University Discussion Paper no. 710 (February 2003); and Sarit Cohen-Goldner and M. Daniela Paserman, "The Dynamic Impact of Immigration on Natives' Labor Market Outcomes: Evidence from Israel," London, Centre for Economic Policy Research (CEPR) Discussion Paper no. 4640 (September 2004).
34. Personal interview, September 2011.
35. On Russian neo-Zionism and the ideological value split in the FSU immigrant community in Israel see Vladimir (Ze'ev) Khanin, "The Jewish Right of Return: Reflections on the Mass Immigration to Israel from the Former Soviet Union," in *Exile and Return: Predicaments of Palestinian Arabs and Jews*, ed. Ian Lustick and Ann Lesch (Philadelphia: University of Pennsylvania Press, 2008), 183–203.
36. For details see Vladimir (Ze'ev) Khanin, "The Israeli 'Russian' Community and Immigrants Party Politics in the 2003 Elections," *Israel Affairs* 10, no. 4 (2004): 162–4.
37. See Yair Ettinger, "'New' Generation Shaking Up Israel's Ultra-Orthodox Political Scene," *Haaretz*, October 28, 2012.

The Transmigration of Media Personalities and Celebrities to Politics: The Case of Yair Lapid

Rafi Mann

School of Communication, Ariel University, Ariel

The electoral success of Yair Lapid's *Yesh Atid* party in the 2013 Knesset elections is discussed in this article as a test case of a worldwide phenomenon of celebrities, among them media personalities, who enter the political field. Bourdieu's interpretive research framework regarding symbolic and social capitals, as well as media capital, is used here to analyse Lapid's versatile career and celebrity status as the background to his performance during the campaign and his ability to win 19 seats in the Knesset. The article also places Lapid's case in the context of political and social developments in Israel in the last decades.

The 2013 national elections in Israel brought to the public's attention the phenomenon of media personalities and celebrities turned politicians more than ever before. The most prominent among them has been Yair Lapid, a popular newspaper columnist, TV anchorperson, interviewer and author. His newly formed party *Yesh Atid* ('There is a Future') won 19 seats in the 120-member parliament. Following the elections, *Yesh Atid* became a major partner in Benjamin Netanyahu's coalition with Lapid nominated as Minister of Finance.

Lapid's celebrity status was predominantly mentioned as one of the explanations for the party's achievement.[1] His electoral success is therefore dealt with here in the context of the globally known phenomenon of media personalities and celebrities turned politicians. The linkage between a celebrity's skills and advantages and Lapid's performance as a candidate is examined based in part on Bourdieu's interpretive research framework regarding symbolic capital and social capital, as well as the later developed concept of media capital. Symbolic capital, according to Bourdieu, includes elements like prestige, charisma and charm,[2] and is a form of power which is not perceived as power or as based on formal authority, but provides legitimization to demands for recognition, deference, obedience or the services of others.[3] Social capital refers to the aggregate of resources which are linked to acquaintances and networks and groups which provide their members' credentials.[4] Media capital, according to

Davis and Seymour, is the accrual of status and other advantages acquired by the ability to use the media in order to communicate with various audiences, both within the political field and with the wider citizenry.[5]

The analysis of Lapid's symbolic, social and media capitals would enable us to shed light on the way his perceived persona was identified by 16% of the voters as the preferred answer to the public's concerns and yearnings. It would also indicate how Lapid's persona fit well into the political field following decades of the personalization, mediatization, commercialism and celebritization of Israel's public sphere. This is in addition to several other processes, among them the continuing crisis of traditional parties; the weakening of the loyalty of voters to their old parties; the growing disappointment of the Israeli public from the country's political and economic systems which has led to a yearning for a 'New Politics' or 'Non-political' leadership; and the effects of the 'social justice' protests of summer 2011.

The analysis of Lapid's electoral performance contributes to the study of Israel's political culture and contemporary history.[6] Beyond the Israeli arena, it is a test case which adds to the growing research field on the role of celebrities in society in general and celebrities turned politicians specifically. As almost no archival material is available yet for researchers about the campaign, most of the information used in this article is based on reports published in Israeli and foreign media. The biased nature of at least some of the reports must be taken into account, but they provide an accumulative corpus which enables us to see how Lapid was presented, directly and indirectly, to the voters.

The article's scope is defined by issues related to Lapid's advantages as a media personality and celebrity. Therefore, it does not deal with other significant elements which affected the election's outcome, including the performance of the other parties and candidates. It should be emphasized as well that the article focuses on Lapid's electability, rather than his performance as an elected politician following the election. This latter aspect should be a subject of another study, only after a considerable time period.

The mediatization, personalization and celebritization of the political field

In the pre-television era, when media was mostly print journalism, the phenomenon of journalists turned politicians was widely known.[7] A '[j]ournalistic career remains one of the most important paths to professional political activity', noted Max Weber in 1919, in his renowned lecture 'Politics as a Vocation'.[8] Countless journalists took that path. In Britain, for example, both Benjamin Disraeli in the nineteenth century[9] and Winston Churchill[10] in the twentieth century practised journalism before they entered parliament. In early 2013, at least three members of the British cabinet were former print or television journalists, as well as a number of prominent members of the opposition Labour Party.[11] Four of the Commonwealth of Australia's 27 prime ministers were ex-journalists and many other former media personalities served as ministers in the federal government or in the federation's various states.[12] In South Korea's 2002 National Assembly, Korea's parliament, 13% of the 299 members were journalists turned politicians. During election times, political parties try to recruit media personalities as candidates, as their name recognition and popularity are assets on the way to the ballot.[13]

Within the wide research field of politics–media relations, much attention has been given in recent decades to the mediatization of politics, a process in which political institutions are increasingly dependent on and shaped by the mass media.[14] The revelation of the media's wide-ranging impact on politics was depicted by Mazzoleni in 1995 as the 'Copernican revolution of political communication', as 'yesterday everything circled around the parties, today everything circles around, and in the space of, media'.[15] Other scholars explored the ways in which the media's logic – professional values and practices – infiltrated the political scene.[16] Meyer went further by claiming that the media had colonized politics and created a 'media democracy'.[17]

The media itself had gone through two major processes: the turning of television, including TV news, into a revenue-driven market, and the blurring of boundaries between news and entertainment.[18] The result was the personalization and celebritization of the news: over-emphasis on personal stories, preferably about celebrities, and the turning of anchor persons, correspondents and interviewers into 'celebrity journalists'.[19]

The prominent role of celebrities in entertainment, sports, marketing, media and politics has led to extensive research on this subject. In his seminal work, Boorstin defined a celebrity in 1961 as 'a person who is known for his well-knownness', created by the media in the context of 'pseudo-events'.[20] In the twenty-first century, Gabler contested Boorstin's portrayal of the celebrity as a symptom of cultural degradation, proposing to see it as a 'dominant art form', in which celebrities' narratives refract many of the basic concerns of the culture.[21]

Much of the scholarly discourse has been devoted to the negative effects of the combined mediatization and celebritization of politics. In the words of Weiskel, 'as the news media have become part of the entertainment industry, entertainment celebrities have entered politics'.[22] West and Orman warned in 2002: 'If we don't take back the celebrity politician system, citizens might well face a political contest between a basket-ball player versus a football player, or a comedian versus rock star, or a movie star versus a television situation comedy star.'[23] Most of the critics have emphasized the degradation of the public and political discourse as style and image replacing substance.[24] Others have seen it as another legitimate expression of representation in a modern democratic society.[25] Most of the studies of celebritization of politics focus on politicians who adopt celebrities' gestures and celebrities who promote political, social or environmental issues.[26] Much less has been written about celebrities who run for elected office, most notable of them being Ronald Reagan and Arnold Schwarzenegger.[27]

Bourdieu's writings regarding symbolic and social capital were adopted as an interpretive research framework for several studies on politics. Among others,

Jarvis tracked the symbolic capitals of parties in the US,[28] and Davis applied Bourdieu's framework to the study of mobility in the British political field.[29] Davis and Seymour developed Bourdieu's original concept into a new definition of media capital.[30]

Journalists and early celebrities in Israeli politics

In the Zionist movement, media in the form of journalism was associated with political activity from the start. Theodor Herzl was a writer and editor for the Viennese daily *Neue Freie Presse* and kept this job throughout his tenure as leader of the Zionist movement and until his death.[31] The juxtaposition of political activity and writing was based on the great importance attached to the written word in the Jewish tradition, as well as in political movements since the eighteenth century.[32] Max Nordau, Nachum Sokolov, David Ben-Gurion, Zeev Jabotinsky, Berl Katznelson, Moshe Sharet and Zalman Shazar are just a few of many others whose articles were seen as an integral part of their political activities.

Following independence, this synergy did not cease. In 1950, eight out the 11 Hebrew Israeli dailies were published by political parties or by the Histadrut, the largest trade union.[33] As part of the press–politics alliance, 13 out of 120 members (10.8%) of the First Knesset (elected in 1949) were journalists, most of them writers or editors in the parties' newspapers. Ten journalists were members of the second and third Knesset, 11 in the fourth, 10 in the fifth and eight in the sixth Knesset.[34]

The political map and the organizational structure of most parties in the 1950s and 1960s were mostly in line with the Zionist political tradition brought over from Eastern Europe. Most of the Knesset's members were either veteran members of their parties or functionaries of parties and affiliated organizations. Doors were opened, quite rarely, to well-known new recruits, in order to attract voters. The celebrities of the time were people with a record in their professional fields, mainly in the military or culture.

In most cases, such prominent recruits were high-level army officers. Moshe Dayan's name appeared on Mapai's list for the 1949 elections while still in active service. Dayan preferred to stay in the Israel Defence Forces (IDF), and was elected to the Knesset only in 1959, after serving as the army's chief-of-staff. Reserve generals Yegal Alon and Moshe Carmel were members of the Knesset from Achdut Ahavoda. Ezer Weitzman joined Begin's Herut immediately after leaving the army in 1969.

To a lesser extent, parties enlisted noted literary writers. Author Yizhar Smilansky (S. Yzhar) was asked to join Mapai's list in 1949. The party needed his name and reputation as a young and respected writer to counter Mapam, which heralded its wide support of most of the Palmach generation's young prominent authors and poets.[35] For Herut, acclaimed poet Uri Zvi Greenberg served in the first Knesset. There was at least one case in those years in which the media's exposure promoted the election of a new, young parliamentarian: in 1965 Shulamit Aloni was included in the Maarach list, mainly due to her popular pioneer radio programme *Beyond the Working Hours* which was devoted to citizen and consumer rights.[36]

Yet such fresh political faces were not seen often. The reluctance of the parties' leaders and bureaucrats to allow new candidates onto their lists was identified in 1977 by Weiss as one of the reasons for the traditional parties' decline.[37] This observation was made in the decade in which the series of gradual changes which occurred in both the political system and the Israeli media came to the fore. In politics, many of the traditional parties whose roots were in Zionist political movements in Eastern Europe were weakening. The decline of those parties coalesced with the growing sense of public mistrust of traditional leadership following the Yom Kippur War.

From a closed system to an open political field

The aftershock of the Yom Kippur War not only brought about the fall from power of the Labour party in May 1977. It also introduced a new era in Israel's politics, one in which new parties took power from the traditional political organizations. In an unprecedented fresh injection to the political system, the newly formed Dash ('Democratic Movement for Change') became the third largest party with 15 seats in the Knesset.[38]

The transition from the almost closed party system of the 1950s and 1960s to an open political field continued through the 1980s, with new parties emerging, among them the Sephardi religious Shas. It accelerated in the 1990s with the introduction of a new election law, which enabled the direct election of the Prime Minister. Though the direct election of the Prime Minister was short-lived (it was in effect in the 1996, 1999 and 2001 elections, before the Knesset repealed the law[39]) it had at least two long-term implications: First, it gave Israeli voters a greater degree of choice than ever before, and freed many of them from their previous party loyalties. Second, it intensified the process of personalization of the political arena, which has directed most of the public attention toward the leader rather than the party and its policies.[40] This personalization grew, as more parties adopted primaries as the preferred mechanism for electing their candidates to the Knesset.[41] Both the direct election of the Prime Minister and the parties' primaries signalled the increased Americanization of Israel's politics,[42] as well as the mediatization of that field.[43]

One of the results of those processes was the opening of the political field to new participants – new parties as well as new candidates. New parties were formed in some cases by politicians who left their old parties to form new alliances, like Mifleget Hamerkz (the Centre Party) in 1999 or Ariel Sharon's Kadima (Forward) in 2005. In other cases, such novel parties were formed by new players, many of them without any previous political experience, as happened with the Pensioners Party, which won six seats in 2006, only to disappear in the following elections. As for new candidates, they included celebrities like Pnina Rosenblum, a model, actress and businesswoman, who served as a Likud member of the Knesset for a few months and was ridiculed by a columnist as 'trash celebrity'.[44] Quite a few of the newcomers were media personalities, among them Shelly Yachimovitz, who rose within a few years to the leadership of the Avoda Party, Nitzan Horowitz, Uri Orbach, Micky Rosenthal, Merav Micaeli and others. One of the most notable members of this group was Yair Lapid's father, Josef (Tommy) Lapid, a senior writer for Maariv, playwright, author of highly popular tour guide books, host of a weekly radio programme and a combative and provocative television panellist. In 1999, he became a politician and led the Shinui party to two electoral successes: six seats in the Knesset in 1999 and 15 in 2003, only to disintegrate before the 2006 elections.

Yair Lapid's symbolic, social and media capital

Yair Lapid's (born 1963) symbolic capital has been accumulated over three decades of a varied career. During his military service, he was a correspondent for the IDF weekly Magazine *Bamachane* ('In the camp'). Later, he joined the staff of *Maariv* as a reporter and then as a copy-editor at the paper's news desk, an editor of the daily supplement and a columnist. In 2002 he joined *Yedioth Aharonoth*, where his personal column was prominently placed as the opening text of the paper's weekly magazine, which has been the country's highest circulation publication. In retrospect, he used the hundreds of columns he had published throughout the years as an equivalent of a personal political platform. 'There is no other politician in Israel, as senior as he is, whose views were spread out in front of the public, so widely and precisely', he wrote as he announced his crossover to politics.[45] Concurrently he authored a few books, wrote lyrics for leading Israeli singers, appeared in Israeli films and was the screenwriter of two television series.

His television career started in 1994, as the host of Friday evening's main programme on public channel 1. From 2000 to 2007 he hosted his weekly television interview programme *Yair Lapid* on commercial channel 2. From 2008 until 2012 he was the anchorman of Channel 2's weekend magazine show *Ulpan Shishi* (Friday's studio).[46] His television career extended to the US, where he served in the late 1990s as the head of the television division in Arnon Milchan's *New Regency Productions*.[47]

In 2003, Lapid was named the celebrity face of Israel's largest bank, Bank Hapoalim, and served as its public presenter and endorser for five years. The bank's choice may have helped to decipher his appeal to the voters a decade later, in defining elements of Lapid's symbolic capital. Studies indicate that a celebrity-endorser is chosen by a company to promote its product on the bases of his or her public recognition, being liked by the public as uncontroversial and trustworthy, as well as being a cultural symbol who reflects the values and ideas of a particular culture.[48] Although we are not privy to the internal deliberations between the bank's management and its advertising agency, it would be fair to assume that these were some of their criteria in choosing Lapid.

Lapid's role as a bank presenter was one of the expressions of the 'media revolution' of the 1990s.[49] As the media was turning into a predominantly revenue-driven market, the commercialization had an effect on journalists as well. Like popular culture or sports celebrities, their celebritization was accompanied by commodification, as some of them began to appear in commercials.[50] Some journalists criticized this phenomenon as unethical professional behaviour, but in the period's spirit, representing a bank might even strengthen Lapid's public image as a respectable public figure who was well rewarded for his qualifications.

Based on Gabler's emphasis of the essential narrative component of a celebrity,[51] the bank decision to be represented by Lapid corresponded well with one of his most popular themes – 'Israeliness'. In his columns and on television, he often delineated the components of being an Israeli: the feelings, the gestures, the traumas and various other elements of that supposedly communal experience. Other writers often criticized Lapid's attempts to construct an artificial and imaginary collective identity in a highly divided society.[52] But his columns on this subject became popular reading material in schools, youth movements and in the military, adding another component to his symbolic capital.

The 'Israeliness' concept was an important element of Lapid's symbolic capital for the bank, as it would be in politics: not only an optimistic message of unity, but also perceived as apolitical. In his column 'Why I am going into politics' in 2012, he forcefully rejected any attempt to brand him as 'right-wing' or 'leftist', and defined himself as 'an Israeli patriot, Jew and Zionist'.[53]

Studies of prominent popular culture celebrity turned politicians, among them Ronald Reagan, indicate other relevant components of Lapid's symbolic capital. One is the element of musicality, which, according to Marshal, politicians and celebrities utilize as a hegemonic cultural symbol to craft these public personalities.[54] Part of Lapid's image has been constructed with masculine symbols, among them his Thai boxing hobby, cigars and frequent mentions of Hemingway as a source of inspiration.[55]

His professional style, mostly on television, enabled Lapid to publicly project important elements of Bourdieu's definition of symbolic capital – prestige, charisma and charm. This was apparent, for example, in the interviews he conducted with politicians in his highly rated programme *Yair Lapid* prior to the 2006 elections. Karniel and Lavie-Dinur found that the intimate atmosphere created by Lapid in those interviews gave the politicians an opportunity to display their more personal, emotional side.[56] Lapid's style as an interviewer was always non-combative and his guests could always anticipate sympathetic conversations, conducted by the 'handsome charismatic host'.[57] This style helped him foster his image as a public figure known for 'his handsome face and his pleasant temperament and his charming persona'.[58] Such interviews, according to Eltheide, blur the line separating journalists from their interviewees.[59] These friendly encounters thus enriched Lapid's symbolic capital by enhancing his prestige as a prominent media personality courted by the country's leaders and able to converse with them on an equal footing.

Lapid has been endowed with another quality which had been identified by Marshal as a requirement for both entertainment celebrities and politicians: the ability to project solidarity with the public. 'Just as entertainment celebrities share embarrassing family stories and discuss their hobbies to appear more personable, politicians must construct performances highlighting their connection with "everyday" Americans', wrote Marshal.[60] Lapid had chronicled his private daily life often in his newspaper columns, in a way which enabled his readers to identify with him.

The ability to project a sense of solidarity with the public was a significant element in Lapid's efforts to portray himself as the candidate who would carry the spirit of the 2011 summer of social protest into the political field better than the others. At the height of the protest, Lapid published a front-page article in *Yedioth Aharonoth* titled 'The Slave Rebellion'. It was a direct address of empathy and support with 'my brothers, the slaves', Israel's middle class, which was singled out by Lapid a year later as the main target of his campaign. 'We are not socialist, my brothers the slaves, yet we know how to identify injustice when we see it. Israel's middle class is paying for those below it, and that's fine, but also for those who are above it, and that's very wrong', Lapid wrote.[61]

Despite his sympathy and full identification with the middle class, Lapid was careful not to write the article in first person. This can be attributed to another important element of his symbolic capital: his ability to project a dual impression as to his place between various spheres. This is a common strategy adopted by both celebrities and politicians, who, in the words of McKernan 'must master a performance that simultaneously portrays them as unique and ordinary'.[62] Lapid therefore has branded himself as the leader of the middle class struggle, without hiding that fact that economically he had done better than most voters. He is a prominent public figure who feels at ease with ministers and tycoons, but can spend evenings in a modest popular public singing bar; he is well connected to the most prominent politicians, but at the same time he marketed himself as a new kind of politician. As an interviewer and anchorman, he played an important political role even before entering the political field – but tried to convince voters that he would not act like all other politicians.

Presenting a new kind of politics was a crucial component of Lapid's campaign from the start, in branding himself as a 'non-politician', an outsider. He repeated the slogan of 'New Politics' and the sweeping promise 'to change the system and get rid of the old, corrupt politics'.[63] Canon, who studied the influx of 'amateur politicians' to the USA Congress, attributed the success of candidates with no previous elective experience to their ability to portray themselves as 'running against Washington'. This plays well in societies where citizens are suspicious of career politicians, and tend in many cases to support a candidate who is branding himself as somebody who is not 'one of those'.[64]

Lapid's marketing of 'newness' corresponded with the Israeli public's widespread mistrust and negative sentiment towards politicians and the political system, as indicated by the findings of *The Israeli Democracy Index 2012*: only 33.8% of the Jewish population trusts political parties and 52.9% the Knesset.[65] This attitude was manifested publicly in the early 1990s, when mass protests were held in front of the Knesset under the slogan *Mushchatim nimastem!* ('We're fed up with you corrupt people!').[66]

In order to position his party as a clear antithesis to the old politics, Lapid decided that Yesh Atid's list would not include any politician who had been elected in the past at the national level. Since he needed people with political and executive experience, he drafted in other public figures, among them two mayors. Such local politicians are considered more connected to the grass-roots than national figures. Additionally, he chose representatives of civil society from a wide range sectors. Out of the 19 elected members of the party, there are eight women, two moderate rabbis and two members of the Jewish Ethiopian community.[67]

However, representatives of civil society, whose presence on the list reflected the zeitgeist following the 2011 protest, could be only part of the overall list of a party whose leader aimed from the beginning to take part in government. There was a need to also incorporate experienced figures who would boost Yesh Adit's credentials and respectability in the central fields of national security and economics. Former head of ISA (Shaback – Israel Security Agency) Yaakov Perry, who joined the list, brought with him senior-level business and financial experience as Cellcom's president and as chairman of Mizrachi Bank. Another security expert on the list was former senior police officer, Mickey Levy.

The list's fabric was an adoption of the successful strategies of both media organizations in which Lapid had worked prior to his crossover to politics. *Yedioth Aharonoth*, which brands itself as 'the country's newspaper', and ratings leader Channel 2 pride themselves on their ability to reach almost all sectors and classes in Israeli society. Previously, his professional style was well synchronized with those two organizations, whose appeal to the largest audiences was based on their ability to identify the wider common denominator and to refrain from taking any radical positions. As a candidate, Lapid adopted some elements of these strategies to his centrist game plan, especially regarding the central issue of relations with the Palestinians and the future of the territories held by Israel since 1967. This was done alongside his choice of the slogan 'Where is the money?', which echoed the frustration of most of the Israeli population, although he decided to focus his efforts specifically on the middle class.

It should be remembered though that definitions of 'the country' or Lapid's 'Israeliness' do not include two large components of Israel society: the Ultra-Orthodox Jews and the Arabs, who together comprise almost one-third of the state's citizenry.

A significant component of Lapid's electoral success should be attributed to his media capital. According to Davis and Seymour, such capital is based on an accumulation of knowledge about how news production works and journalists operate.[68] Most politicians accumulate such capital gradually through their political careers, or by heavily relying on communication advisers and consultants. Unlike them, media-savvy Lapid entered the highly mediatized political arena after his varied and long professional experience.

Alongside his use of traditional media, he adapted himself easily to the new media, and made extensive use of social media. His American consultant, Mark Mellman, ascribed some of Lapid's success to the decision to invest a major part of the party's resources on the internet, which enabled him to have inexpensive, reciprocal, popular and up-to-date communication with the public.[69]

His media capital consists not only of knowledge and understanding of the media's logic, but also close acquaintance with leading journalists, as well as publishers and directors of influential media organizations. *Yedioth Aharonoth* is often dubbed in the media as 'Lapid's home paper'.[70]

Lapid's case corresponds well with Bourdieu's concept of social capital in more than one aspect. One of the credentials which contribute to one's social capital is the family name and connections.[71] Not only was his father, Tommy Lapid, a well-known figure in media and politics. Yair Lapid's mother, Shulamit Lapid, was a renowned author. His grandfather, David Gilady, was one of the founders of *Maariv* and served as senior writer of the newspaper at the time when it was the highest circulation newspaper.

Being the son of a media personality-turn-politician familiarized Yair Lapid in advance with the road he was about to take. 'I walk in the shadow of my father', he said before the elections, 'but I also learn from his mistakes'.[72] One of the lessons from his father's meteoric but short political career was that one cannot just rely on positive press and TV appearances. While Tommy Lapid dismissed the need for party branches, infrastructure and organization in the age of mediatized politics,[73] his son's campaign was not based exclusively on traditional or new media. Under the command of Brigadier-General (res.) and high-tech businessman Hillel Kobrinsky, the party had established 103 braches around the country with some 15,000 volunteers.[74] One of their missions was to arrange meetings for him with people all over the country, based on the assumption that face-to-face encounters are an essential addition to messages transferred by mass communication. Interviews with voters a few days after the elections proved the effectiveness of such meetings. 'I met him and he impressed me as a trustworthy person, I like him … He touched me … He is young and handsome', voters were quoted as saying.[75]

Some prominent figures in Lapid's network were his late father's friends, among them former Prime Minister Ehud Olmert and the late journalist and author Amnon Dankner. But throughout his career, Yair Lapid created an elaborate social network of his own. Its contribution toward his election was not merely symbolic and was reviled shortly after the election when the list of his financial supporters was made public. Aside from donors, a group of 79 business persons in the finance, real estate and high-tech sectors provided NIS 9.2 million in financial guarantees to his party collectively.[76] In addition, journalists and producers who worked with him were ready to join the campaign and played an important role both publicly and behind the scenes.

Conclusion

The article examined Lapid's 2013 electoral success as a test case of the political and sociological phenomenon of celebrities and media personalities turned politicians. Various studies of this subject in other countries provided the background on which it can be concluded that many of Lapid's ingredients for success were linked to the symbolic, social and media capital he had accumulated throughout his career in media and popular culture. Lapid's celebrity status was a crucial and important part of his success, but it needed to be augmented by an effective organization, a respectable list of candidates and other elements. In the wider context, Lapid's success was an outcome of the various developments and processes within Israeli society and politics since the 1970s. He was able, more than other candidates, to capture the zeitgeist by presenting the image of a 'non-political politician' and to take advantage of the public's disappointment with the political system.

This article was written a few months after Yair Lapid was appointed Minister of Finance and presented the government's budget, which encountered sharp criticism from many of his supporters. Future studies should analyse his performance as an active politician and as a minister. In particular, it should answer the question whether his symbolic, social and media capital, which helped paved his way to the Knesset and cabinet, are as relevant to his performance there.

Another question waiting to be answered in the future is whether Lapid's success in obtaining a large number of seats in the Knesset could be repeated, or would Yesh Atid disintegrate or even disappear like Dash, Shinuy, Kadima, the Pensioners Party and other 'fashionable' or 'atmosphere' parties. The answer depends not only on Lapid's performance, but on the political culture, in which a politician who presented himself as a 'non-politician' may find it difficult to repeat his success after years in the Knesset and the cabinet. This is especially so when a candidate was elected as a celebrity – a status which develops quickly, and can crumble just as quickly.[77]

Disclosure statement

No potential conflict of interest was reported by the author.

Notes on contributor

Rafi Mann is a senior lecturer in the School of Communication at Ariel University.

Notes

1. See, among others: Isabel Kershner, "Charismatic Leader Helps Israel Turn Toward the Center," *The New York Times*, January 22, 2013, http://www.nytimes.com/2013/01/23/world/middleeast/yair-lapid-guides-yesh-atid-party-to-success-in-israeli-elections.html?_r=0 (accessed August 5, 2013); Raffi Berg, "Profile: Yair Lapid, Israel's Yesh Atid Party leader," *BBC News*, March 14, 2013, http://www.bbc.co.uk/news/world-middle-east-21158464 (accessed August 5, 2013); Harriet Sherwood, "Israel Election Result Hands Rising Star Yair Lapid a Pivotal Role," *The Guardian*, January 23, 2013, http://www.theguardian.com/world/2013/jan/23/israel-election-results-yair-lapid (accessed August 5, 2013).

2. Pierre Bourdieu, *Language and Symbolic Power* (Cambridge, MA: Harvard University Press, 1991), 155.

3. David Swartz, *Culture and Power: The Sociology of Pierre Bourdieu* (Chicago: University of Chicago Press, 1997), 44.

4. Ibid., 75.

5. Aeron Davis and Emily Seymour, "Generating Forms of Media Capital Inside and Outside a Field: the Strange Case of David Cameron in the UK Political Field," *Media, Culture & Society* 32, no. 5 (2010): 739–59.

6. Referring to the possible pitfalls of historiography of present time, the editors of the *Journal of Contemporary History* wrote in its first issue: "Distance in time helps us to see historical events in wider perspective and thus adds an important dimension to our understanding; but distance in time also involves remoteness, lack of immediacy, difficulty in understanding the quality of life of the period that is hard to describe and define, but which may be as important as all the documents in the archives". "Editorial Note," *Journal of Contemporary History* 1, no. 1 (1966): iv.

7. Wayne Errington and Narelle Miragliotta, "From the Gallery to the Parliament: Journalists in the House of Representatives and Senate, 1901–2007," *Australian Journal of Politics & History* 55, no. 4 (2009): 533.

8. Max Weber, *Weber: Political Writings*, ed. Peter Lassman and Ronald Speirs (Cambridge: Cambridge University Press, 1994), 334.

9. Michael Flavin, *Benjamin Disraeli: The Novel as Political Discourse* (Brighton: Sussex Academic Press, 2005), 7.

10. Geoffrey Best, *Churchill: A Study in Greatness* (London: Continuum, 2001), 82.

11. Michael Goldfarb, "Are Journalists What's Wrong with Britain?," *Global Post*, January 5, 2013, http://www.globalpost.com/dispatch/news/regions/europe/united-kingdom/130104/britain-journalists-politicians-politics-economy (accessed April 1, 2013).

12. Errington and Miragliotta, "From the Gallery," 534; Shelley Savage, "Media Politician Bob Carr and the Familiar Path from Journalism to Politics" (paper presented at the Australian Media Traditions Conference, Old Parliament House, Canberra, 24–25 November, 2005).

13. *Press Reference*, South Korea, http://www.pressreference.com/Sa-Sw/South-Korea.html (accessed March 14, 2013).

14. Gianpietro Mazzoleni and Winfried Schulz, "'Mediatization' of Politics: A Challenge for Democracy?," *Political Communication* 16, no. 3 (1999): 247.

15. Gianpietro Mazzoleni, "Towards a Videocracy? Italian Political Communication at a Turning Point," *European Journal of Communication* 10, no. 3 (1995): 308.

16. David Altheide, "Media Logic and Political Communication," *Political Communication* 21, no. 3 (2004): 293–6.

17. Thomas Meyer and Lewis P. Hinchman, *Media Democracy: How the Media Colonize Politics* (Cambridge: Polity Press, 2002).

18. James Hamilton, *All the News That's Fit to Shell: How the Market Transforms Information into News* (Princeton, NJ: Princeton University Press, 2004): 163, 216.

19. David Marshall, "Intimately Intertwined in the Most Public Way – Celebrity and Journalism," in *Journalism: Critical Issues*, ed. Stuart Allen (Maidenhead: Open University Press, 2005), 27.
20. Daniel Boorstin, *The Image: A Guide to Pseudo-Events in America* (New York: Atheneum, 1961), 58.
21. Neal Gabler, *Toward a New Definition of Celebrity* (Los Angeles: Norman Lear Center, 2001), http://www.learcenter.org/pdf/Gabler.pdf (accessed January 1, 2014).
22. Timothy Weiskel, "From Sidekick to Sideshow – Celebrity, Entertainment, and the Politics of Distraction," *American Behavioral Scientist* 49 no. 3 (2005): 393–409.
23. Darrell West and John M. Orman, *Celebrity Politics* (Upper Saddle River, NJ: Prentice Hall, 2003), 119, quoted by John Street, "Celebrity Politicians: Popular Culture and Political Representation," *The British Journal of Politics & International Relations* 6, no. 4 (2004): 435.
24. Mark Wheeler, "The Democratic Worth of Celebrity Politics in an Era of Late Modernity," *The British Journal of Politics & International Relations* 14, no. 3 (2012): 407–22.
25. Street, "Celebrity Politicians," 435–52.
26. Ibid.; David Marsh, Paul Hart, and Karen Tindall, "Celebrity Politics: The Politics of the Late Modernity?," *Political Studies Review* 8, no. 3 (2010): 322–40.
27. Marsh et al., "Celebrity Politics," 324.
28. Sharon Jarvis, *The Talk of the Party: Political Labels, Symbolic Capital, and American Life* (Oxford: Rowman & Littlefield, 2005).
29. Aeron Davis, "Forms of Capital and Mobility in the Political Field: Applying Bourdieu's Conceptual Framework to UK Party Politics," *British Politics* 5, no. 2 (2010): 202–23.
30. Davis and Seymour, "Generating Forms." 744.
31. Rafi Mann, "Herzl and the Press: From the 'Sword of Steel' to Cable Newspaper" [in Hebrew], *Kesher* 21 (1997): 20–36.
32. Jabez D. Hammond and Erastus Root, *The History of Political Parties in the State of New York: from the Ratification of the Federal Constitution to December, 1840*, vol. 1. (Cooperstown: H. & E. Phinney, 1846), 279.
33. Mordechai Naor, *Ladies and Gentlemen, the Press: Chapters in Written Communications in Eretz Israel* [in Hebrew] (Tel Aviv: Ministry of Defence, 2004), 230–40.
34. Asher Zidon, *Knesset: The Parliament of Israel* (New York: Herzl Press, 1968), 337; "Album of the Delegates of the Second Knesset" [in Hebrew] (Tel Aviv: Yedioth Aharonoth, n.d.). The exact count of journalists or ex-journalists in the Knesset is not complete. Some members of the Knesset have identified themselves as journalists, despite the fact that they were just guest columnists.
35. Rafi Mann, *The Leader and the Media: David Ben-Gurion and the Struggle over Israel's Public Sphere 1948–1963* [in Hebrew] (Tel Aviv: Tel Aviv University and Am Oved, 2012), 276.
36. Ada Cohen, "A Voyage from the Home to the Knesset," *Ma'ariv*, November 12, 1965.
37. Shevach Weiss, *The Knesset: Its Functioning and Output* [in Hebrew] (Tel Aviv: Achiassaf, 1977), 55.
38. Elections to the Ninth Knesset results, http://www.knesset.gov.il/description/eng/eng_mimshal_res9.htm (accessed April 20, 2013).
39. Emanuele Ottolenghi, "The 2006 Election and the Legacy of the Direct Election System," *Israel Affairs* 13, no. 2 (2007): 455–75.
40. Peter Van Aelst, Tamir Sheafer, and James Stanyer, "The Personalization of Mediated Political Communication: A Review of Concepts, Operationalizations and Key Findings," *Journalism* 13, no. 2 (2012): 203–20.

41. Gideon Rahat and Tamir Sheafer, "The Personalization (s) of Politics: Israel, 1949–2003," *Political Communication* 24, no. 1 (2007): 65–80.
42. Myron Aronoff, "The 'Americanization' of Israeli Politics: Political and Cultural Change," *Israel Studies* 5, no. 1 (2000): 92–127.
43. Yoram Peri, *Telepopulism: Media and Politics in Israel* (Stamford, CA: Stamford University Press, 2004); Orit Galili, *The Tele-Politicians* [in Hebrew] (Tel Aviv: Ramot, 2004).
44. Barbara Sofer, "The Human Spirit: Stop Pnina-bashing," *Jerusalem Post*, December 23, 2005, http://www.jpost.com/Opinion/Columnists/The-Human-Spirit-Stop-Pnina-bashing (accessed August 20, 2013).
45. Yair Lapid, "Why Am I Going to Politics," *Yedioth-Ahronoth-Shiva Yamim*, January 13, 2012, 2–21.
46. "Yair Lapid," *Ynet Encyclopedia*, http://www.ynet.co.il/yaan/0,7340,L-2338958-MjMzODk1OF8zNDAzMzI3ODZfMTQ4Njg3MjAw-FreeYaan,00.html (accessed August 16, 2013).
47. Nir Natan, "Hollywood Reporter: Yair Lapid to Head New Regency TV Division," *Globs*, January 28, 1997 (accessed August 15, 2013).
48. James Culbreath, "A Cross-Cultural Look at Celebrity Sports Endorsement" (master of business thesis, Auckland University of Technology, 2012).
49. Peri, *Telepopulism*, 26–7.
50. Kerry Ferris, "The Sociology of Celebrity," *Sociology Compass* 1, no. 1 (2007): 371–84.
51. Gabler, *Toward a New Definition*, 5–8.
52. Ron Mayberg, "Yair Hachi-Tov," *NRG*, May 18, 2005, http://www.nrg.co.il/online/5/ART/935/396.html, (accessed September 5, 2013).
53. Lapid, "Why Am I Going to Politics," 21–3.
54. David Marshall, *Celebrity and Power: Fame in Contemporary Culture* (Minneapolis: University of Minnesota Press, 1997), 217.
55. Rotem Starkman, "From 'Mr. Israeli' to Leader of the Middle Class, in 400 Weekly Columns," *Haaretz*, January 24, 2013, http://www.haaretz.com/opinion/from-mr-israeli-to-leader-of-the-middle-class-in-400-weekly-columns.premium-1.496208 (accessed August 20, 2013).
56. Yuval Karniel and Amit Lavie-Dinur, "2006 Elections in Israel: Marking the End of an Era for the Controlled Televised Election Campaign Broadcast," *Journal Media and Communication Studie* 2, no. 2 (2010): 29–38.
57. Ibid., 35.
58. Ari Shavit, "Yair Lapid under Fire," *Haaretz*, May 9, 2013, http://www.haaretz.com/opinion/yair-lapid-under-fire.premium-1.520037 (accessed September 1, 2013).
59. David Altheide, "Media Logic and Political Communication," *Political Communication* 21, no. 3 (2004): 294.
60. Marshall, *Celebrity and Power*, quoted by Brian McKernan, "Politics and Celebrity: A Sociological Understanding." *Sociology Compass* 5, no. 3 (2011): 193.
61. Yair Lapid, "Israel's Slave Rebellion," *Yedioth Ahronoth*, July 20, 2013, http://www.ynetnews.com/articles/0,7340,L-4097856,00.html (accessed August 10, 2013).
62. McKernan, "Politics and Celebrity," 197.
63. "Lapid: Ministers Who Voted for 'Lapid Bill' are Shameless," *Ynetnews*, February 26, 2012, http://www.ynetnews.com/articles/0,7340,L-4195095,00.html (accessed March 30, 2013).
64. David Canon, "The Year of the Outsider: Political Armatures in the U.S. Congress," *The Forum* 8, no. 4 (2011): 1412; David Canon, *Actors, Athletes, and Astronauts: Political Amateurs in the United States Congress* (Chicago: University of Chicago Press, 1990), 3.

65. Tamar Hermann et al., *The Israeli Democracy Index 2012* (Jerusalem: The Israel Democracy Institute, 2012), 42–3, http://en.idi.org.il/media/1365574/Index2012%20-%20Eng.pdf (accessed August 25, 2013).
66. Rafi Mann, *It's Inconceivable* [in Hebrew] (Or-Yehuda: Hed Artzy, 1998), 166–7.
67. Gabe Fisher, "All the Kingmaker's Men, and Women," *The Times of Israel*, January 23, 2013, http://www.timesofisrael.com/yair-lapids-sends-a-diverse-quality-slate-to-knesset/ (accessed September 5, 2013).
68. Davis and Seymour, "Generating Forms," 744.
69. Chemi Shalev, "U.S. Strategist's Formula for Lapid's Stunning Success: the Candidate, the Message, and the Internet," *Haaretz*, January 27, 2013, http://www.haaretz.com/blogs/west-of-eden/u-s-strategist-s-formula-for-lapid-s-stunning-success-the-candidate-the-message-and-the-internet.premium-1.496705 (accessed March 25, 2013).
70. Yossi Verter, "With New Budget, Yair Lapid Has Become the Victim of His Own Rhetoric," *Haaretz*, May 10, 2013, http://www.haaretz.com/weekend/with-new-budget-yair-lapid-has-become-the-victim-of-his-own-rhetoric.premium-1.523311 (accessed August 23, 2013).
71. Pierre Bourdieu, "Forms of Capital," in *Readings in Economic Sociology*, ed. Nicole Woolsey Biggart (Malden, MA: Blackwell, 2002), 286.
72. Sari Makover-Blikov, "Lapid Yair Lapid," *Maariv-Sofshavua*, January 4, 2013, 16–26.
73. Vered Levy-Barzilay, "Get Off My Back, Evil People," *Musaf Haaretz*, December 5, 2005, http://www.haaretz.co.il/misc/1.1064923 (accessed February 25, 2013).
74. Shuky Sade, "Yair and Lihi Feel that They Owe Everything to Hillel," *Marker Weekly*, February 8, 2013, 10–12.
75. Oded Shalom, "Lapid's Races," *Yedioth Ahronoth – Hamusaf Leshabat*, January 2, 2013, 14–15.
76. Moti Bassok, Eytan Avriel and Zvi Zrahiya, "Business Figures Personally Backed Loans for Yesh Atid's Knesset Campaign," *Haaretz*, March 27, 2013, http://www.haaretz.com/business/business-figures-personally-backed-loans-for-yesh-atid-s-knesset-campaign.premium-1.511940 (accessed April 1, 2013).
77. Charles Kurzman et al., "Celebrity Status," *Sociological Theory* 25, no. 4 (2007): 363.

'New politics', new media – new political language? A rhetorical perspective on candidates' self-presentation in electronic campaigns in the 2013 Israeli elections

Eithan Orkibi

Department of Sociology and Anthropology, Ariel University

Political campaigns running during the Israeli general elections of 2013 saw a rapidly growing use of new media. According to reports, most of the electronic campaign activity focused on candidates' or their respective party's Facebook page. This article explores the rhetorical dimensions of electronic campaigns and particularly focuses on the formation of the public image of three candidate, all of whom were identified with the promise of a 'new politics': Yair Lapid, head of the newly formed 'middle class party' Yesh Atid; Shelly Yachimovich, head of the Israeli Labour Party; and Naftali Bennett, newly elected head of the religious Zionist party, Habayit Hayehudi. The rhetorical analysis uncovers three discursive strategies used by all three candidates: informality, meta-textuality and narrativity. These discursive strategies transform the campaign microblogs into personal 'campaign diaries' used by the candidates to account for 'behind the scenes' anecdotes, impressions and insights. The analysis shows that candidates used personal Facebook microblogs to strengthen their image as authentic and complex characters, rather than mediated personas engineered by campaign managers. This article argues that such political images were strategically designed in order to support the campaigns' promise to break from the 'old politics' and warrant the candidates' commitment to the 'new politics'.

New politics, new campaign language?

Political analysts, journalists and pundits debated constantly during the 2013 Israeli elections the fact that 'for the first time, the election campaign was not about strategic or social-civil issues'.[1] Some claimed that other than ideology, it was mostly about the 'candidates' personalities'.[2] Others suggested that it was essentially about 'change', and that both the election campaigns and their results proved that 'The public was fed up not only with the prime minister, but with the whole political system. The public showed last night that it wanted to see new faces, no matter what they stood for'.[3] Partially inspired by the 2011 protest movement,[4] this desire for 'change' was reflected by promises for 'new politics', which – to sum up some of the campaigns' messages – would diminish the traditional divide between 'left' and 'right' in Israeli politics, redefine 'public interest' through open deliberation in the public sphere, constitute new relations between 'voters' and 'politicians' and favour 'general interest' over partisan loyalties: 'Voters had their say in a clear voice, and expressed an unambiguous preference: enough with the old politics, long live the new politics – transparency, accountability, backing your promises and prioritizing principles, not seats'.[5]

For many observers, the spirit of new politics, as an omnipresent buzzword which swept through the election campaign, was evident in what was perceived as new political communication trends. For starters, it was understood that 'new politics uses new media', and therefore candidates who ground their campaign on the rejection of the 'old politics', also reject the 'monologue style associated with the old propaganda style' in favour of 'a dialogue with the public' using social networks.[6] Indeed, the use of new media during the 2013 general elections was much higher than ever before. According to reports, most of the electronic campaign activity focused on candidates' personal Facebook pages or that of their respective party, alongside YouTube channels and Instagram and Twitter accounts, though to a lesser extent.[7] Another new trend was described as 'new language':

> It is not a matter of Ideology, but rather of language. It is the language of a generation that was shaped by the information revolution of the 1990s.... It's the language of the people who stroll with their kids on Saturday and upload a picture on Facebook.... It's an open code language. You can write it to the right, as did Naftali Bennett. You can write to the center-left, like Yair Lapid. It brings the politician closer to the ordinary people.[8]

The purpose of this article is to explore the rhetorical dimension of this 'new language' in election campaigns. It will particularly focus on the personal presentation of three prominent candidates associated with the 'new politics': Yair Lapid, head of the newly formed 'middle class party' Yesh Atid, who championed 'New Politics' as his central slogan and main agenda during his campaign; Naftali Bennett, newly elected head of the religious Zionist party Habayit Hayehudi (previously known as Mafdal), whose election slogan was 'Something New Begins'; and Shelly Yachimovich, head of the Israeli Labour Party (HaAvoda), which absorbed many of the leaders of the 2011 social protest. The study offers a systematic analysis of the personal Facebook pages of each candidate, aimed at capturing the constitutive elements of this 'new language', its role in political marketing in general and in the formation of each candidate's image in particular.

'Hetero-attributed' and 'self-attributed' candidate image

Candidate image in election campaigns is an established area of investigation in scientific literature in the realm of political psychology focusing on voter behaviour and candidate evaluation,[9] as well as in the field of political communication.[10] In an era of mediated politics and political marketing, the cliché that 'candidates are marketed as well as soap'[11] cannot be easily dismissed. Though the simplistic notion of the 'candidate as a bar of soap' has been profoundly challenged by communication scholars and political scientists,[12] it is still widely acknowledged that 'how a political candidate looks and speaks has a significant impact on that candidate's chances of being elected'.[13] For the purpose of this article, let us consider Kenneth L. Hacker's definition of the term 'candidate image' as 'clusters of voter perceptions of candidates'.[14] This definition stresses the dynamic relations between campaign messages and the public evaluation of a candidate. Simply put, images strategically conveyed by the campaign managers, together with those diffused by media coverage, are interlaced with voters' pre-existing, evolving and contextualized impressions and transform into cognitive representations of candidates.

In terms of the content involved in the creation of a candidate's image,[15] scholarship points to two closely related but nonetheless distinct categories. The first could be described as 'politician attributes' – namely the candidate's traits associated with the common perception of a politician or leader, the most fundamental of which are, as Balmas and Sheafer note,[16] competence, leadership, power, intelligence, credibility and morality. Studies that investigate the relations between candidate attributes and campaign issues, as well as character valance and policy platform, correlate the two, suggesting that politicians' attributes and a candidate's position on relevant issues are linked in the process of voters' impressions and candidate image formation.[17] Another category could be described as 'personal attributes', which relates to the various characteristics of the candidate as an individual person. Located somewhere between the voter's perception of the candidate as a private person and his or her human characteristics is what Bruce Buchanan refers to as politicians' 'way of being themselves'.[18] Personal attributes could be traced, to use Allan Louden and Kristen McCauliff's categorization of image variables, in the projected personal qualities of the candidate, such as temperament, goodwill and devotion to family and spouse, as well as communicative behaviour, such as humour, sensitivity, friendliness and physical appearance and attractiveness.[19]

A politician's attributes, and to some extent his/her personal character-istics, are usually mediated by a third party: they are constructed by the media or strategically primed by campaign managers through discursive genres such as opinion pieces in newspapers, testimonies, biographies or advertisements. In this type of message, it is other people, such as pundits, colleagues, opinion makers or anchors, who present the candidates and discuss their merits. In contrast, personal attributes – and in particular communicative behaviour – are mostly visible in candidates' *self-*presentation. Personal qualities such as sociability, attentiveness, humour, friendliness, and so on, are more traceable in discursive genres in which the candidate himself transmits the message, or, simply stated, when the candidate talks. Discursive genres such as speeches, interviews, debates or weblogs expose target audiences to both campaign messages and candidates' distinctive modalities for delivering their messages: language, style, manners and conduct, voice and appearance.[20] As a result, a distinction could be drawn between a 'hetero-attributed' and 'self-attributed' candidate image: in the former, the candidate's image is mostly constructed by a third party, while in the latter the information allowing for the construction of the candidate's image comes directly from the candidate.

Rhetorical *ethos* in candidate image formation

Scholars have previously hinted at the relevance of the rhetorical notion of *ethos*, character in Greek, to the study of candidate image.[21] In his fundamental treatise on rhetoric, Aristotle places the speaker's character among the three most important rhetorical devices, together with the logical argument (*logos*) and the emotional appeal (*pathos*). The Aristotelian concept of *ethos* refers to a central rhetorical exigency imposed on speakers in any given situation: securing the persuasive efficiency of their speech by portraying themselves as reliable and credible. Aristotle classifies three specific traits that, once projected within the confines of speech, confer credibility to the speaker: *phronesis*, *arete* and *eunoia*,[22] meaning wisdom, moral character and goodwill. In the Roman tradition of rhetoric, the notion of character considers prior knowledge about the speaker, such as public reputation and social status, as important constituents of the speaker's image, together with his/her style of discourse, such as fluency, elegance and eloquence.[23] Although the concept of character and rhetorical *ethos* has over the centuries been the subject of many interpretations, the basic Aristotelian principle remains relevant. As Marshall W. Alcorn put it: 'often it is not a person's *ideas* but a person's *character* that changes people... When people identify with a speaker, they can be manipulated into accepting the speaker's ideas and values'.[24]

In modern rhetorical theory, *ethos* is mostly associated with the notion of credibility, and the term *ethos* is frequently replaced by 'source credibility',[25] suggesting that the perceived credibility of the speaker is composed of factors such as trustworthiness, competence and objectivity,[26] or authoritativeness and goodwill.[27] But *ethos* is not merely an instrument of persuasion, allowing speakers to promote a positive image of themselves (while challenging the image of their opponents, as demonstrated in the political contest). Above all, the various attempts to measure and assess source credibility view *ethos* as a *perceived* construct – namely, as the 'attitude toward a source of communication held at a given time by a receiver'.[28] In other terms, *ethos* is strategically constructed by speakers to meet their target audiences' social values, expectations and costumes. In this sense, as Alan Brinton notes, the *ethos* of a (good) orator is in fact a credible reflection of the society's general character. Such *ethos* makes a (good) speaker appear as 'one whom we can trust to express our shared values, to think in terms of our common assumption, to exercise good judgment, and to speak for us'.[29]

But how is *ethos* actually constructed? In her seminal essay on the presentation of self in language, Ruth Amossy discusses *ethos* in terms of the 'discursive image of self', asserting that *ethos* is far more complex than just projecting an image in support of a claim. In fact, it is a continuous discursive practice related to social activities such as institutional positioning, legitimizing one's discourse in a competitive public sphere, identity formation, and so forth.[30] From a discursive standpoint, *ethos* can be viewed as verbal identity. This approach does not neglect the persuasive function of *ethos* as a distinct device in rhetorical communication. Rather, it considers *ethos* as an important constituent of any discourse, whether purely argumentative (i.e. seeking adherence to a specific argument) or less argumentative (i.e. informative, literary, entertainment and so on).

The French tradition of discourse analysis and argumentation suggests at least two dimensions to *ethos*: the spatial-temporal dimension and the textual dimension. The spatial-temporal dimension establishes a distinction between the *discursive ethos* and a *pre-discursive ethos*. Similar to the Aristotelian concept, discursive *ethos* is defined as that which is projected by the speaker in his or her speech, in the confines of a given discourse. Pre-discursive *ethos*, akin to the Latin tradition, consists of prior knowledge about the speaker. This knowledge might reflect the speaker's reputation or the impressions remaining following previous encounters with the speaker. In addition, pre-discursive *ethos* might result from shared ideas or ready-made images and stereotypes related to the social category or group with which the speaker is affiliated.[31] Thus, pre-discursive *ethos* is basically the accumulated knowledge that the audience might have about the speaker, whether directly related to the speaker's personality or to social representation of the speaker's affiliations. It is assumed that by strategically designing his or her discursive *ethos* in a given situation, the speaker might confirm, modify or completely transform his or her pre-discursive *ethos*.[32] The textual dimension establishes a distinction between two modalities for conveying *ethos*, which might be explicitly employed by the speaker,[33] as speakers often talk about themselves, disclosing emotions, evoking their merits and credentials, openly affirming their qualities and abilities. When not asserted, *ethos* is implied,[34] or rather shown: a specific lingo or jargon, a unique discursive behaviour, a linguistic style which reflect one's personality in a given situation. Speakers thus assert *ethos*, yet they also show it as proof of their genuine character or affiliation with a specific social category or group.

Candidate image and rhetorical *ethos* are closely related concepts, but one distinction should be emphasized: while candidate image is in itself a primary goal of the communication process (it constitutes the claim sent to audiences), rhetorical *ethos* is a representation of self which 'aims at obtaining or reinforcing the adherence of the audience to some thesis',[35] and not an independent message. This distinction implies that when analysing persuasion in electoral campaigns one should not consider *ethos* as the rhetorical equivalent of the term 'candidate image', but should rather explore the modalities through which the rhetorical *ethos* of the candidate supports the claim to the 'candidate image'. If rhetorical *ethos* 'reinforces adherence' to a series of claims, then one should examine the functions and contributions *ethos* makes to the effective transmission of the messages in the candidate's campaign, which include, as previously stated, the candidate's public image.

Israeli candidates' presentation of self in microblogs

This article focuses on the self-attributed candidate image in the 2013 Israeli election campaign. As such, it explores the rhetoric of presentation of self in the discursive realm which allows for – or effectively simulates – a direct communication between the candidates and their target audiences, with no apparent third-party interference. For this purpose, the analysis follows the Facebook accounts belonging to three candidates, over a period of three months prior to Election Day (22 October 2012–21 January 2013).[36] A systematic analysis of their posts and statuses over this period has enabled the identification and demonstration of three prominent rhetorical conventions used throughout the three electronic campaigns: the usage of informal language, meta-textual remarks and narratives.

Informality

Candidates' status updates on Facebook tend to adopt an informal, casual and even spontaneous communication style, which emulates daily interaction. This informality manifests lexically, through the embracing of a 'familiar' or 'casual' language register and in the recurring use of informal expressions. A notable example is Yachimovich's habit of opening her status updates with 'Hi, it's Shelly', thus identifying herself by her first name and greeting her readers with 'Hi', which is reserved in Hebrew for intimate and friendly interactions and is rarely used in public or official contexts. The discursive formula 'Hi, it's Shelly' is culturally perceived as a familiar greeting form used for a phone call with a friend or family and is therefore associated with oral rather than written communication. Similarly, Naftali Bennett constantly refers to his readers as 'My brothers', an address form generally associated with vernacular language or military slang, in which 'brother' (*Achi*) is a fellow combatant. When used in interactions with strangers, the expression 'brother' is utilized to generate a sense of intimacy and stimulate a sentiment of solidarity among metaphorical brothers, or, in our case, fellow Israelis and/or Jews.

However, informality goes beyond the selection of words and expressions associated with daily interactions amongst friends and peers. It also governs the timing and topics of status updates. This dimension of informality is evident in the random and unpredictable frequency of updates, which ranges from several every day to a just a few per week. Furthermore, the timing of these 'casual' status updates makes them seem incidental, as they often digress from the campaign's core themes. Yachimovich, for instance, posted on 8 January 2013, during a particularly rainy week, a picture of her dog at the Tel Aviv beach with the caption: 'our old dog Luna is excited about the weather. Here she is during her morning stroll on the deserted seashore at the end of my street'. In other cases, timing may be less arbitrary, but the status will focus on a minor detail relating to an important event. For example, on 9 January Yachimovich posted a picture of a rainbow taken from her car window during the previously mentioned rainy week, noting that 'I just took this picture on my way to Bat-Hefer, where houses and factories were flooded. We will meet with the Regional Council Chief'. While Yachimovich used a casual comment to inform her reader that she was on her way to visit a region damaged by the storm, Bennett utilized the stormy weather on the evening of 8 January in order to share his thoughts about the 'thousands of IDF combatants who are guarding us in the cold, rain, wind and snow. Let them have a huge warm like!' In many cases, the seemingly casual status update might evoke a personal event or address, an issue unrelated to the campaign or the political agenda, such as sports or popular culture. Yair Lapid updated his readers about his 49th birthday on 5 November, while Naftali Bennett shared his admiration for a contestant on a prime-time television singing contest just one month before the elections (16 December), stating: 'there are sometimes those songs or people you simply can't resist. It happened to me yesterday. On Saturday night the young Ofir Ben-Shitrit performed with a pure voice and displayed a charming personality. I had to share it with you'.

The informality, demonstrated in the choice of words, topics and timing, creates the impression that the candidates' status updates are irrelevant to the party agenda or the schedule of the official campaign. Many updates convey no political message per se and consist of personal remarks and comments about the popular topics on the social networks. In fact, these informal posts are often seen as spontaneous unedited comments that were not part of the official campaign's public relations policy. The informality simulates the interaction between friends and thus facilitates a new perspective on the 'official campaign' by distinguishing 'official' from 'informal'; a distinction between the standard, processed and carefully designed messages coming from the official campaign, and the personal, raw and casual status updates.

Meta-textuality

The electronic campaign discourse contains a large amount of meta-textual (or meta-discursive) utterances – i.e. remarks and comments in which the candidate describes, evaluates or reflects on his or her own speech. These seemingly introspective meditations by the candidates on the textual content of their own production further accentuates the perceived distinction between the 'official campaign' in the field and the alternative communication channel online. Two weeks prior to election day, on 8 January, Yair Lapid noted in a status update that 'we are very fortunate to be living in the era of social networks, as we can talk about what really matters'. When his son was drafted into the Israel Defence Forces, on 12 December 2012, Lapid uploaded a photograph of his son standing at the entrance to the IDF recruitment centre with the caption: 'This is not a political post. This is my boy joining the army. In fact, it just might be a political post all the same.'

Therefore, meta-textual remarks are often used to characterize an electronic campaign as a unique, unmediated and liberated platform for communication, which facilitates a continuous interaction in which processes of meaning production and sense-making are transparent and accounted for. In other cases, meta-textual remarks address the campaign itself, by way of depicting personal, if not private impressions, thoughts and experiences from the official campaign activity. Natfali Bennett, for instance, comments on many activities and constantly posts statements exposing his experience as a political candidate, such as this post published on 11 December after a Hanukkah celebration with a group of supporters:

> We had such an amazing day today. [. . .] For those of you who think that an electoral campaign is frustrating – you're wrong. It's wonderful. It allows you to get in touch with the Israeli nation, to meet new people and visit old places.

When Yair Lapid posted a celebratory remark on 29 November, to celebrate reaching 100,000 followers on Facebook, he noted that he enjoys travelling across the country, because 'nothing can replace the personal contact with people you meet along the way'. He then added that 'New politics means new instruments [i.e. social networks] with which one can communicate directly with so many people', and concluded that 'it is always interesting to converse with you about our future'. Lapid compares his online interactions to personal meetings with voters, thus portraying an image in which his Facebook persona is the very same Yair Lapid one would meet in person.

Lastly, meta-textual remarks are used to convey the perception of a transparent process of message making. The perceived reflexivity exposes not only the campaign's dynamics by listing detailed description of various activities, but also the motives and logic which justify different persuasive manoeuvres. This convention is typically employed when debating online with competing candidates: Each candidate lays out his or her arguments and simultaneously explains his or her rhetorical moves. An example of such an occurrence took place a month before the elections, when Yachimovich and Lapid debated over the Israeli water supply system and costs. It started with a post by Lapid on 16 December, in which he criticized Yachimovich's inability to promote reform due to her commitment to the trade unions. In return, the Labour party candidate refuted her opponent's accusations and put forward her own arguments in a status posted on 18 December:

> You may have noticed by now that I usually criticize and confront Netanyahu, Lieberman and Steinitz, but this time I must address Yair Lapid's status regarding the issue of water supply. His status was full of particularly hilarious factual errors.

The very next day, Lapid replied by owning up to his factual mistakes:

> I double-checked. She was right and I was wrong. This too is part of the New Politics – you made a mistake? Come forward, apologize and stand corrected. And now that we know that there is no shame in admitting your mistakes, when will she admit that her economic programme is based on inaccurate numbers?

Meta-textuality thus acts as an additional layer of interpretation, in which the candidates outline their personal perspective on the 'official campaign', characterize their own 'e-campaign' as an exclusive platform for indirect interaction with their supporters and expose the mechanism that produces the message. As result, candidates' status updates on Facebook are coupled with the 'official campaign' as a supplement, much like audio commentary on DVDs, thus disclosing additional information to the readers and providing them with access to the 'making of' the campaign, as seen and described by the candidate's point of view.

Narrativity

The political candidates' online discourse is rich with narratives and anecdotes, as well as descriptions of scenes and various interactions. In addition to the informative discourse (i.e. providing information about activities and developments) and the declarative discourse (i.e. statements, comments and assertions), a narrative mode of discourse provides the candidates with the capability to expose a vast range of sentiments, motives and associations. As storytellers, candidates reveal their emotions, values and cultural background and present themselves as rounded characters.

These constructed narratives are primarily mobilized to promote moral arguments. This is mostly true in the case of Naftali Bennett, whose Facebook account is particularly rich with tales and fables that are not necessarily related to the campaign or to his political agenda, but rather taken from Jewish tradition and Israeli folklore. Nonetheless, all of them lead to conclusions relevant to Bennett's campaign. Among his many 'tales of the week' or 'fables for Shabbat', one can read the 'charming little tale' of Rabbi Aryeh Levin in the 3 January 2014 post. Levin, an important figure in the religious faction of the Israeli revisionist movement, once approached a young soldier who had become non-religious and stopped wearing a yarmulke: 'You have a big and kind heart and that's what counts. You are also a soldier placing your life at risk for all of us in Israel. Please drink tea with me; your yarmulke is probably bigger than mine', he said. The political significance of this story highlights military service as a core value and primary civil duty, thus it places itself in the folkloric tradition and the collective memory.

While Naftali Bennett uses narratives as arguments, Yair Lapid uses tangible scenographic descriptions deeply rooted in the Israeli cultural imaginary in order to promote his own messages. In a status posted on 14 December, Lapid addressed inequality in society regarding military service, opening with a depiction of a common event in a typical Israeli family: 'Friday noon. It's that time when our children come home from the army... except for those the government released from duty because our old politicians are too scared of the Ultra-Orthodox parties.' Lapid thus adopts a narrative discourse in order to contextualize his political message and insert it into prevailing social representations of contemporary Israeli reality.

In addition to the packaging of the campaign messages in narrative form, the narrative mode of discourse is used to frame the entire campaign as a serial narrative, in which each status serves as a contiguous chapter. The campaign is dramatically structured as a series of events leading toward a climax and closure. This can be seen, for instance, in Shelly Yachimovich's status of 16 January, reporting on the results of a poll held at the University of Haifa: 'Hi, it's Shelly. We won the polls at the University of Haifa. By large margin [...] This victory continues an impressive series of victories we've been having in campuses across the country.' Her linear narrative form performs a rhetorical function similar to an *ad-populum* argument: namely, it uses the (supposed) growing popularity of the candidate as an appeal to the majority. As a rhetorical device, this form becomes an element within the candidate's campaign efforts to create a 'bandwagon effect' (i.e. attracting voters through an apparent momentum) or to evoke 'horse race' terminology (i.e. create the impression that one side is beginning to gain ground and the race is coming to an end). Yachimovich employed such tactics in status updates that aimed to synthesize a strong sense of a potential turning point as the electoral campaign reached its final stages. On 18 January she wrote: 'Look at the polls. They prove that the elections are not over yet. The gap between the blocs is closing. It may be difficult, but it is not impossible, to replace Netanyahu.'

Candidates' microblogs as a personal campaign diary

As stated above, in addition to practical information about the ongoing campaign activities and daily messages, the candidates' microblogs on Facebook offer a comprehensive description, in the first person, of the candidate's experience of the campaign. The discursive characteristics of the candidate's electronic campaign – informality, meta-textuality and narrativity – shape a reading experience similar to reading a personal diary. Resembling other forms of personal writing, such as travel logs or personal diaries, the posts are not informative but are rather interpretative – they give access to the author's personal viewpoint and subjective perspective with regard to an 'objective' reality. Indeed, for many critics, weblogs of various sorts descend from the literary genre of the personal diary, which, since the sixteenth century, is defined by three characteristics: writing about the present, writing periodically in consecutive chapters and accounting for the writer's personal experience.[37] As noted by Carolyn Miller and Dawn Shepherd, it is the salient personal perspective which constitutes the cultural resemblance between diaries and blogs in general and shapes the reading experience of the blog as a chronicle of the writer's reflections and thoughts.[38] It appears that weblogs are increasingly appreciated as a legitimate genre of self-representation, and, as van Dijck notes in his discussion on weblogs as a form of diary writing, it is precisely the selection of words, the style and the cultural references that 'give away a person's character' and constitute the weblog as an efficient form of self-representation.[39]

As in other types of autobiographical writing, candidate's microblogs imply a unity between the author, narrator and protagonist, all of which lead back to the candidates themselves. Together with the real-time production–consumption practice – i.e. reporting of events as they occur or immediately afterwards – candidates' microblogging is rhetorically designed to be consumed as a genuine depiction of 'reality'[40] and, consequently, as a more authentic representation of the candidate's personality.[41] This effect of relative reality is evident in the literary field, when renowned authors turn to autobiographical writing, thus exceeding their institutionalized position as 'storytellers' and reveal their genuine self. In the same way, I would argue that campaign microblogging facilitates a similar transgression, as candidates shift from their institutionalized role as engineered products of political marketing, and enter a discursive space where they can engage in a seemingly non-staged or authentic interaction. In this sense, microblogs are not just a privileged platform for the candidates to present themselves as part of the political marketing process; they also support the continuing personalization process in political communication in Israel[42] and in other media-saturated democracies.[43]

The discursive features of the candidates' microblogs – informality, meta-textuality, narrativity – appear as a departure from the carefully staged media events and the polished advertisements. As such, they provide the blog with a certain degree of credibility (they *appear* authentic), and mark the candidate as a legitimate agent in the discursive space of the social networks. This discursive behaviour warrants the distinction, frequently asserted by the candidates, between the 'official' or 'standard' campaign and communication through the social network. Such a distinction dictates the reading experience and assigns roles: while the 'official' campaign's target audience remains a passive receiver of a persuasive message, the consumer of the electronic campaign becomes an engaged agent. In addition to the interactive nature of social networks, the very act of 'following' a candidate (even without sharing or replying), constitutes the reader as a committed addressee who interacts with the candidate willingly, or, at the very least, becomes part of a distinct group with which the candidate communicates 'naturally', as a real person, in a peer-to-peer exchange or friend-to-friend interaction.

The rhetorical *ethos* of the 'expert citizen'

From a rhetorical viewpoint, candidates' microblogging can be defined as meta-campaign discourse. It fulfils a communicative function far more complicated than providing an additional platform for the diffusion of campaign messages, or establishing an alternative venue for interaction with supporters. Firstly, in an era of growing cynicism and scepticism regarding political marketing, which is closely associated with 'old politics',[44] political candidates' microblogs seem to warrant the content of the 'official campaign'. They enable effective communication between candidates and audiences, by portraying the candidate as a rounded character, rather than a mediated persona whose public image is strategically designed by campaign managers. As such, candidates' microblogs do not constitute an entirely new realm for political communication, nor do they undermine or obviate the content of the 'official' campaign. In fact, the centrality of self-representation in candidates' microblogs suggests that their unique contribution to the general campaign is related to the securing of an authentic candidate image, rather than to the diffusion of political messages per se.

Secondly, candidates' online discourse evokes an image of a political agent who is well suited to an era of 'new politics'. Portraying themselves as genuine members of the discursive field which is mostly identified with the 'new politics' and repeatedly demonstrating their discursive skills and know-how, the candidates posit themselves not as politicians who adjust themselves to a new political culture, but rather as politically engaged citizens on a mission to conquer and reform the political institution. To the extent that 'new politics' is about 'citizen's politics',[45] a mixture of citizen-led activism and an anti-politics sentiment, microblogs could be described as the primary arena wherein candidates can construct their rhetorical *ethos* as an 'expert citizen',[46] to use Henrik Bang's term. In their discussion on new forms of political participation, Bang, followed by Yaojun Li and David Marsh,[47] use the term 'expert citizen' in order to refer to professionals working in voluntary or civil society organizations. But the *ethos* of such expert citizens transcends an institutional position: it encompasses the features associated with contemporary civil engagement, including one's motivation for political activism, a genuine commitment to social change, long-established dialogue skills, networking capabilities and media competence, as well as a pragmatic willingness to collaborate with allies inside the political system.[48] Thus, both in style and in content, microblogging on social networks such as Facebook secures the candidate's *ethos* of expert citizen, and rhetorically warrants the campaign promise of engaging in a 'new politics'. Candidates' self-presentation online thus shapes their images not as worthy politicians, but rather as prominent members of the civil society who deserve the trust of their potential voters.

Acknowledgements

This research was supported by the Institute for the Study of New Media, Politics and Society in the School of Communication at Ariel University. I would like to warmly thank Hayne Krakover for her precious assistance with gathering the primary sources for the analysis.

Disclosure statement

No potential conflict of interest was reported by the author.

Notes on contributor

Eithan Orkibi is a lecturer in the Department of Sociology and Anthropology at Ariel University, and a member of the ADARR (Analysis of Discourse, Argumentation and Rhetoric) research group, Tel Aviv.

Notes

1. Nadav Eyal, "The Choice to Weaken the Emptiness," *Ma'ariv*, January 20, 2013, 2. See also Akiva Eldar, "What Was the Israeli Elections Really About?," *Al-Monitor*, January 23, 2013, http://www.al-monitor.com/pulse/originals/2013/01/israeli-election-about.html (accessed April 15, 2013).
2. Shalom Yerushalmi, "The Main Thing is the Participation," *Ma'ariv*, January 22, 2013, 4.
3. Sima Kadmon, "A Vote for the Future," *Yedioth Ahronoth*, January 24, 2013, .4.
4. See Uri Ram and Dani Filk, "The 14th of July of Daphni Leef: The Rise and Fall of the Social Protest" [in Hebrew], *Theory and Criticism* 41 (2013): 17–43.
5. Sever Plotzker, "A Responsible Adult Needed," *Yedioth Ahronot – Mamon*, January 26, 2013, 1.
6. Baruch Leshem and Yehiel Limor, "Yair Lapid and Facebook: New Politics and New Media," Israel Public Relations Association website (n.d.), http://www.ispra.org.il/%D7%99%D7%90%D7%99%D7%A8-%D7%9C%D7%A4%D7%99%D7%93-%D7%95%D7%94%D7%A4%D7%99%D7%99%D7%A1%D7%91%D7%95%D7%A7-%D7%A4%D7%95%D7%9C%D7%99%D7%98%D7%99%D7%A7%D7%94-%D7%97%D7%93%D7%A9%D7%94-%D7%95%D7%AA%D7%A7%D7%A9%D7%95%D7%A8%D7%AA-%D7%97%D7%93%D7%A9%D7%94.html (accessed April 15, 2013).
7. For a detailed assessment and overview, see Sharon Haleva-Amir, "Political Communication: E-Campaigns in the 2013 Israeli Elections," in *Annual Report: The Israeli Media in 2013 – Agendas, Uses and Trends* [in Hebrew], ed. Rafi Mann and Azi Lev-On (Ariel: Ariel University, 2014), 79–90. On e-campaigns during the 2009 Israeli elections, see Sharon Haleva-Amir, "Online Israeli politics: Current State of the Art," *Israel Affairs* 17, no. 3 (2011): 467–85; Azi Lev-On, "Campaigning Online: Use of the Internet by Parties, Candidates and Voters in National and Local Election Campaigns in Israel," *Policy and Internet* 3, no. 1 (2011): 1–28
8. Nadav Eyal, "To Speak in a New Language," *Ma'ariv – Musaf-Shabat*, January 25, 2013, 8.
9. See, for instance, Carolyn L. Funk, "Bringing the Candidate into Models of Candidate Evaluation," *The Journal of Politics* 61, no. 3 (1999): 700–720; Matthew Mendelsohn, "The Media and Interpersonal Communications: The Priming of Issues, Leaders, and Party Identification," *Journal of Politics*, 58, no. 1 (1996): 112–25.
10. See, in particular, Dan Nimmo and Robert L. Savage's path-breaking work from 1976, *Candidates and Their Images: Concepts, Methods, and Findings* (Pacific Palisades, CA: Goodyear, 1976), and both of Kenneth L. Hacker's edited volumes: *Presidential Candidate Images* (Lanham, MD: Rowman & Littlefield, 2004), and *Candidate Images in Presidential Elections* (Westport, CT: Praeger, 1995).
11. To use an expression coined by Philip Kotler and Sidney J. Levy, "Broadening the Concept of Marketing," *Journal of Marketing* 33, no. 1 (1969): 10; for a comprehensive discussion on political marketing and images, see: Dominic Wring, "Reconciling Marketing with Political Science: Theories of Political Marketing," *Journal of Marketing Management* 13, no. 7 (1997): 651–63.
12. For an overview and discussion, see Alex Marland, "Marketing Political Soap: A Political Marketing View of Selling Candidates Like Soap, of Electioneering as a

Ritual, and of Electoral Military Analogies," *Journal of Public Affairs* 3, no. 2 (2003): 103–15.

13. Shawn W. Rosenberg, Lisa Bohan, Patrick McCafferty, and Kevin Harris, "The Image and the Vote: The Effect of Candidate Presentation on Voter Preference," *American Journal of Political Science* 30, no. 1 (1986): 108–27.

14. Kenneth l. Hacker, "The Continued Importance of the Candidate Image Construct", in *Presidential Candidate Images* (see note 10), 4.

15. For a literature overview and discussion on candidate image content and issues–persona relations, see Susan A. Hellweg, "Campaign and Candidate Image in American Presidential Elections," in *Presidential Candidate Images* (see note 10), 21–47.

16. Meital Balmas and Tamir Sheafer, "Candidate Image in Election Campaigns: Attribute Agenda Setting, Affective Priming, and Voting Intentions," *International Journal of Public Opinion Research* 22, no. 2 (2010): 206.

17. See, for example: Kenneth L. Hacker, Walter R. Zakahi, Maury J. Giles, and Shaun McQuitty, "Components of Candidate Images: Statistical Analysis of the Issue–Persona Dichotomy in the Presidential Campaign of 1996," *Communication Monographs* 67, no. 3 (2000): 227–38; Gilles Serra, "Polarization of What? A Model of Elections with Endogenous Valence," *Journal of Politics* 72, no. 2 (2010): 426–37.

18. Bruce Buchanan, "Sizing-Up Candidates," *PS: Political Science and Politics* 21, no. 2 (1988): 251, cited in Allen Louden and Kristen McCauliff, "The 'Authentic Candidate': Extending Candidate Image Assessment", in *Presidential Candidate Images* (see note 10), 85–103.

19. Louden and McCauliff, "The 'Authentic Candidate'," 87. For other examples, see Betty Glad, "Evaluating Presidential Character," *Presidential Studies Quarterly* 28, no. 4 (1998): 861–72; James P. Pfiffner, *The Character Factor* (College Station, TX: A&M University Press, 2004).

20. See: Bruce Bimber and Richard Davis, *Campaigning Online. The Internet in U.S. Elections* (New York: Oxford University Press, 2003); Joanne Morreale, *The Presidential Campaign Film: A Critical History* (Westport, CT: Praeger, 1993); Rebecca Verser and Robert H. Wicks, "Managing Voter Impression: the Use of Images on Presidential Candidate Web Sites During the 2000 Campaign," *Journal of Communication* 56, no. 1 (2006): 178–97.

21. Louden and McCauliff, "The 'Authentic Candidate'," 94; Lynda Lee Kaid, "Measuring Candidate Images with Semantic Differentials," in *Presidential Candidate Images* (see note 10), 323; Dan Nimmo, "The Formation of Candidate Images during Presidential Campaigns," in *Candidate Images in Presidential Elections* (see note 10), 60; Jerry L. Allen and Daniel J. Post, "Source Valence in Assessing Candidate Image in a Local Election," *Communication Research Reports* 21, no. 2 (2004): 176; Leonard Shyles, "Defining 'Images' of Presidential Candidates from Televised Political Spot Advertisements," *Political Behavior* 6, no. 2 (1984): 172.

22. Aristotle, *Rhetoric*, trans. W. Rhys Robert (New York: Random House, 1954), 1337b.

23. For an overview and discussion of the classical concepts of *ethos*, see Roger D. Cherry, "*Ethos* versus Persona: Self-Representation in Written Discourse," *Written Communication* 5, no. 3 (1988): 251–76; S. Michael Halloran, "Aristotle's Concept of *Ethos*, or If Not His Somebody Else's," *Rhetoric Review* 1, no. 1 (1982): 58–63.

24. Marshall W. Alcorn, Jr, "Self-Structure as a Rhetorical Device: Modern *Ethos* and the Divisiveness of the Self", in *Ethos: New Essays in Rhetorical and Critical*

Theory, ed. James S. Baumlin and Tita French Baumlin (Dallas, TX: Southern Methodist University Press, 1994), 3–35.

25. James Jasinski, *Sourcebook on Rhetoric: Key Concepts in Contemporary Rhetorical Studies* (Thousand Oaks, CA: Sage, 2001), 230.

26. Jack L. Whitehead, "Factors of Source Credibility," *Quarterly Journal of Speech* 54, no. 1 (1968): 59–63.

27. James C. McCroskey, "Scales for the Measurement of *Ethos*," *Speech Monographs* 33, no. 1 (1966): 65–72.

28. James C. McCroskey and Thomas J. Young, "*Ethos* and Credibility: The Construct and its Measurement after Three Decades," *Central States Speech Journal* 32, no. 1 (1981): 24.

29. Alan Brinton, "A Rhetorical View of the *Ad Hominem*," *Australasian Journal of Philosophy* 63, no. 1 (1985): 55.

30. Ruth Amossy, *La présentation de soi: Ethos et identité verbale* (Paris: Presse Universitaire de France, 2010).

31. Patrick Charaudeau, *Le discours politique: les masques du pouvoir* (Paris: Vuibert, 2005), 90.

32. Roth Amossy, "*Ethos* at the Crossroads of Disciplines: Rhetoric, Pragmatics, Sociology," *Poetics Today* 22, no. 1 (2001): 11.

33. Such assertions fall into the category of 'ethotic arguments'. See Alan Brinton, "Ethotic Argument," *History of Philosophy Quarterly* 5, no. 3 (1986): 245–58; Michael Leff, "Perelman, Ad Hominem Argument, and Rhetorical *Ethos*," *Argumentation* 23, no. 3 (2009): 301–11.

34. Dominique Maingueneau, "Analysing Self-Constituting Discourses," *Discourse Studies* 2, no. 2 (1999): 194.

35. Chaim Perelman and Lucie Olbrechts-Tyteca, *The New Rhetoric: A Treatise on Argumentation*, trans. John Wilkinson and Purcell Weaver (Notre Dame, IN: Notre Dame University Press, 1969), 11, cited in Amossy, "*Ethos* at the Crossroads," 5.

36. https://www.facebook.com/YairLapid, https://he-il.facebook.com/ShellyYachimovich, https://he-il.facebook.com/NaftaliBennett.

37. Carolyn R. Miller and Dawn Shepherd, "Blogging as Social Action: A Genre Analysis of the Weblog," in *Rhetoric, Community and Culture of Weblogs*, ed. Laura Gurak et al. (2004), http://blog.lib.umn.edu/blogosphere/blogging_as_social_action_a_genre_analysis_of_the_weblog.html (accessed January 15, 2014).

38. Ibid. See also Susan C. Herring, Lois Ann Scheidt, Elijah Wright, and Sabrina Bonus, "Weblogs as a Bridging Genre," *Information Technology and People* 18, no. 2 (2005): 142–71.

39. José van Dijck, "Composing the Self: Of Diaries and Lifelogs," *Fibreculture Journal* 3 (2004): §20, http://three.fibreculturejournal.org/fcj-012-composing-the-self-of-diaries-and-lifelogs/ (accessed January 15, 2014).

40. Lena Karlsson, "Desperately Seeking Sameness: The Processes and Pleasures of Identification in Women's Diary Blog Reading," *Feminist Media Studies* 7, no. 2 (2007): 137–53.

41. Gracie Lawson-Borders and Rita Kirk, "Blogs in Campaign Communication," *American Behavioral Scientist* 49, no. 4 (2005): 548–59.

42. Gideon Rahat and Tamir Sheafer, "The Personalization(s) of Politics: Israel, 1949–2003," *Political Communication* 24, no. 1 (2005): 65–80.

43. Peter Van Aelst, Tamir Sheafer, and James Stanyer, "Personalization of Mediated Political Communication: A Review of Concepts, Operationalizations and Key Findings," *Journalism: Theory, Practice and Criticism* 13, no. 2 (2011): 203–20.

44. Pippa Norris, "Do Campaign Communications Matter for Civic Engagement? American Elections from Eisenhower to George W. Bush," in *Do Political*

Campaigns Matter? Campaign Effects in Elections and Referendums, ed. David Farrell and Rudiger Schmitt-Beck, (London: Routledge, 2002), 127–44.

45. Colin Hay and Gerry Stoker, "Revitalising Politics: Have We Lost the Plot?," *Representation* 45, no. 3 (2009): 225–36.

46. Henrik Bang, "Everyday Makers and Expert Citizens," in *Remaking Governance: Peoples, Politics and the Public Sphere*, ed. Janet Newman (Bristol: Policy Press, 2005), 159–79.

47. Yaojun Li and David Marsh, "New Forms of Political Participation: Searching for Expert Citizens and Everyday Makers," *British Journal of Political Science* 38, no. 2 (2008): 247–72.

48. Ibid., 250.

The 2013 Israeli elections and historic recurrences

Eyal Lewin

Department of Middle Eastern Studies and Political Science, Ariel University

The 2013 election campaign in Israel shows, at first glance, some unanticipated results and unexpected reactions of several political actors. Three events in particular can be noted: (1) the rise of a significant centrist middle-class party; (2) the association of the newly elected right-wing Prime Minister with his left-wing rivals; and (3) the revival of a national religious party after years of decline. A broad overview, however, reveals that from many perspectives numerous key elements of Israeli politics have remained broadly the same over the decades. Some unanticipated outcomes of the elections are to a substantial extent repetitions of past events, referred to in this paper as historic recurrences. In order to establish this claim about historic recurrence, each event is compared to past events with which several striking similarities are found. In order to explain the phenomenon of historic recurrence in Israeli politics, two sets of concepts are applied: the sociological terminology regarding reference group and collective identity, and rational choice theories about voter behaviour and the preferences of political actors.

Students are often intrigued when, in order to demonstrate what comparative studies are about, one analyses historical chronicles that seem to portray similar events, albeit in different settings. One can learn about Napoleon's 1812 invasion of the vast Eastern terrain. One can study his underestimation of the Russian peasants' stubbornness and the hazardous winter that made it impossible to transport food and fodder to supply his troops; we can also read about Mikhail Kutuzov's 'scorched earth' strategy that eventually left very little of the *Grande Armée*.[1]

Similarly one can look at how, in 1941, millions of Wehrmacht soldiers, accompanied by massive Luftwaffe air strikes, implemented their winning *Blitzkrieg* doctrine deep into Soviet territory. One can examine the scorched earth policy that Joseph Stalin enforced, the Russian factories that were dismantled and rebuilt in the eastern parts of Central Asia, and, finally, we can look at the stubborn Soviet resistance along the whole front that eventually slowed down the German attack. The Germans were stopped a mere 30 kilometres away from the Kremlin. There they encountered Katyusha rockets, which had a huge psychological effect, and faced fresh and well-equipped Soviet forces that had been brought in from Siberia and the Far East. Above all, the Germans were faced with the Russian winter that literally froze parts of the German army to death.[2]

One can learn about Woodrow Wilson, who was re-elected president on his promise to keep the United States out of World War I. Yet the Germans' conspiratorial relations with Mexico convinced him to break his word almost immediately, and the US entered the war, and more than 117,000 Americans lost their lives.[3] Discussing broken election promises, one can also study Charles De Gaulle, who as a presidential candidate made a 1958 trip to Algiers where he announced, 'Vive l'Algérie française'. In 1959 De Gaulle was elected president, and in 1961 he decided not to fulfil his promise by giving up Algeria. As a result, in 1962 about 1,000,000 *pieds-noirs* (European Algerians) fled to France in fear of the Front de Liberation Nationale (FLN) (the local Muslim guerrilla forces), which orchestrated violent lynch mobs that massacred tens of thousands of former non-European collaborators who were left behind.[4]

It seems that history, far from being linear, is to a substantial extent cyclical in nature, while social development is achieved through perpetuated patterns of human and organizational behaviour. This paper suggests that Israel's 2013 election campaign can be regarded from this perspective. When first examined, one can identify some unanticipated results and unexpected reactions of several political actors. However a more in-depth overview tells a different story. This broader perspective reveals that many important political aspects have not changed much over decades of Israeli politics. In retrospect, some of the major unforeseen political changes can also be viewed as repetitions of similar political events of the past.

We shall therefore review three major results of the 2013 elections and portray them as historic recurrences: (1) the rise of a meaningful centrist middle-class party; (2) the newly elected right-wing Prime Minister who prefers to associate himself with his left-wing rivals; and (3) the national religious party that had gone into decline, almost disappeared, but then suddenly revived.

Finally, this study offers a sociological explanation based on *reference groups* and *group identity* and also a possible rational theory explanation.

The historic recurrence of the rise of the new centrist middle-class party

The big surprise of the 2013 elections was the success of the Yesh Atid centre party led by former journalist Yair Lapid, which obtained 19 seats and became the second-largest force in the Knesset. This election outcome exceeded all expectations and significantly changed the possible options for the composition of the next government. It was the result of a rising new actor in Israeli politics: the middle class.

Beginning in July 2011, hundreds of thousands of Israeli citizens held demonstrations all over the country, protesting against the cost of living, housing prices, high taxes and the ongoing deterioration of public services. Though initially sparked by issues relating to the cost of housing, the protests expanded to include other issues relating to the social order and power structure in Israel. There was a common rallying cry: 'The people demand social justice!' Whether or not an objective examination would confirm their claims, middle-class Israelis who took to the streets believed that they were the victims of modern capitalism. These were the people who, several months after the protests, would be responsible for a new electoral power that emerged in the ballots: Lapid's centre party Yesh Atid, an optimistic name that translates as 'There is a Future'. As Nahum Barnea, one of Israel's most respected commentators, put it:

> The lesson [of the election] must begin at the protest movement of the summer of 2011. By the time autumn arrived, the tents on the streets had been dismantled; the general sense was that the protest was dead and buried. That wasn't the case. The seeds had been sown. They were waiting for the rain in order to sprout, and the rain came ... The feeling of disgust with the political game rules did not die: it only increased further.[5]

Yael Paz-Melamed, another journalist, analysed Lapid's electoral success, linking the middle-class protests with voter behaviour:

> In the winter of 2013 the biggest protest of all was held. There were not half a million people there as there were in the summer of 2011; rather, it was millions of people. The silent majority in Israel; the people who work, pay taxes, go to the army, serve in reserve duty, and especially those who chose to live here freely – they got off of the couch, filled the ballot boxes and took back the power they deserve.[6]

These accounts certainly correspond with the Yesh Atid political platform that appeals to the middle class. A synopsis of several of these far-reaching ideas is: (1) attaining the right balance between free market principles and a society based on solidarity; (2) promoting free competition and encouraging small business and entrepreneurs; (3) the fair distribution of both economic and military burdens; (4) a change in the system of government, with the aim of establishing efficiency and stability; (5) the writing of a constitution; (6) a fundamental reform that would improve the availability of housing; (7) investment in education; (8) striving for a balance between obtaining peace in the region, through the willingness to make concessions, with the need to constantly maintain Israel's security.[7]

At first glance it seems that, after decades of electoral tie between Israeli right-wing and left-wing political divisions mainly concerning matters of foreign policy, domestic issues finally prevailed and there was a demand for a different kind of politics. The old guard of the right-wing bloc, led by Likud, and of the left-wing bloc, led by Labour, had to give way to a central new political power.

However, as the book of Ecclesiastes says: 'The thing that hath been, it is that which shall be; and that which is done is that which shall be done; and there is no new thing under the sun.'[8] During the 1970s, Israeli citizens took the streets. Rage over political and military failures in the 1973 War led to loss of trust in the political system and to growing public discontent. This was the background for the rapid emergence of Dash (Democratic Movement for Change), a new party that won 15 seats in the Knesset in the 1977 elections.

Dash became very popular from the minute it was founded. It was a centrist party, made up of prominent figures from both the left and the right, from both military and academic circles, and, most important of all, it was a party that based its electoral power partly on the protest movements that sprang up after the war (though one ought to bear in mind a more ideological component, Shinui, that amounted to about 20% of the party's voters).[9] Beyond the desire to tame Mapai's power, the political platform of Dash reflected the party's middle-class voters. A summary of some of its clauses could be as follows: (1) attaining the right balance between free market principles and a society based on solidarity; (2) promoting free competition and encouraging small business and entrepreneurs; (3) advancing equality between sectors and social groups; (4) change of the electoral system in favour of a more stable one; (5) writing a constitution; (6) implementing fundamental reforms that would prioritize the availability of housing; (7) investment in education; (8) striving for peace in the region through both a willingness for concessions and an ongoing maintenance of Israel's security.[10]

The similarity between the two parties, the 2013 Yesh Atid and the 1977 Dash, is anything but coincidental. Long before the founding of Dash, and after, there were other attempts to revive the dormant middle class. The first appearance of a party with a distinct liberal-capitalist character could be traced to the pre-state days of the Zionist Congress as early as the 1930s. Based on social sectors that were shaped decades before the establishment of the state, the General Zionists emerged in 1951 with 20 seats in the Knesset; this party was a centrist political force that tried to break the right–left paradigm of Israeli politics with domestic ideas of economic liberalism, proposals for the formation of a constitution and the notion that peace with the country's neighbours is an essential political goal. Their slogan, clarifying their intention, was 'Let us live here in this country!'[11]

Some of the attempts to revive the liberal-centrist political force throughout the history of Israeli politics were made by Yair Lapid's father, Yosef (Tommy) Lapid. In 1985, he formed a liberal party that failed to enter the Knesset, but later on headed the Shinui (Change) party, a fraction that had survived from the former Dash, achieving six seats in the Knesset in 1999 and rising to 15 seats in 2003.[12]

Ariel Sharon realized early in his political career that the goldmine was hidden in the centre of the political map. Between loyalty to Mapai during the 1950s and becoming the *enfant terrible* of the Israeli right during the 1980s, Sharon was the one who established the Likud party in 1973 by a merger of the right-wing Herut party and the centrist Liberal Party, along with some additional independent elements. Decades later, in 2005, when he sensed that the public was ready for yet another attempt, he founded Kadima, and by doing so managed, for a short while, to reshuffle the pack of cards of Israeli politics.[13] History thus provides a wider perspective on the rising star of Yair Lapid's 2013 electoral success.

The historic recurrence of a Likud leader who allies with former rivals

Another surprising inconsistency was Netanyahu's uncoupling with the Shas ultra-Orthodox party after the 2013 elections. The origins of the traditional partnership between Likud and Shas date back to the 1980s, when Shas was founded. In the 1984 elections, during Shas' initial campaign, Likud gained only 41 seats, whereas Labour won 44 seats. This numerical gap could have technically allowed Labour leader Shimon Peres to form a government. Yet Shas did not even bargain with Labour, and Shas' political leader – the newly elected Knesset Member Itzhak Peretz – immediately referred to the Likud leader Ytzhak Shamir as the next Prime Minister. This was, for several reasons, no coincidence. The ideals of nationalism that characterize Likud's ideology originate from Jewish religious values. Many of the voters who chose Shas from the very beginning were originally traditional Likud as well as Mafdal voters. The decision to stick with the Likud was initially a strategic one, based on the premises that many, and perhaps even most, Shas voters are Likud supporters at heart, who maintain much respect for the since-deceased spiritual leader of Shas, Rabbi Ovadia Yosef, but would vote Shas only once they were convinced that Likud would be about to win the elections in any case. During the 1990s, Likud lost power and Shas partnered with Labour-led coalitions; still, the animosity towards the left and identification with a more nationalistic rationale amongst Shas voters made the Likud–Shas alliance not only a traditional one, but also the most natural bond.[14]

With the 2013 elections results, Netanyahu was able to create a 61-seat bloc founded on the renewal of the right-wing partnership,[15] and then have other potential candidates join him. Yet Netanyahu, for the third time in office and by now the Israeli Prime Minister with the longest term, wanted the one thing he had never really achieved: legitimacy from the middle- and upper-class elites. In order to gain their trust, he had to convince them that he was anything but a right-wing nationalistic extremist. The way to do so was to form a coalition with a centrist party (Yesh Atid), and then add to it those whose sole agenda was peace – at almost any price – namely Hatnua (Movement) led by Tzipi Livni. Now that his old loyalties were dumped and new partners from the centre and from the left strengthened his public legitimacy, Netanyahu could even take a new dovish political stand on Israeli foreign affairs.

The 2013 electoral results indicate just how much history repeats itself and Netanyahu's post-2013 election political behaviour is, in a sense, a repeat of Menachem Begin's political conduct 36 years earlier. The May 1977 elections marked a dramatic turnover, with Likud forming, for the first time, a governmental coalition. After decades of ideological rivalry – and what some Labour party leaders considered to be no less than a catastrophe – change had finally taken place: Menachem Begin, the extreme right-wing leader who was regarded by some of his counterparts as a former terrorist, came to power. From an objective point of view, one cannot blame Begin's opponents for overestimating his firm stand on foreign policy matters. Ever since the 1969 campaign and until 1996, the political platform of the Likud declared that the goal of the State of Israel should be Jewish sovereignty over Greater Israel – with borders that included all territories acquired during the 1967 War: Judea, Samaria, the Jordan Valley and the whole Sinai Peninsula. Already in 1973 the territorial issue was the major dispute between Labour and Likud; whereas Labour platforms called for a compromise in which Israel would give up its control over the densely populated West Bank and Gaza, Likud's policy, following Menachem Begin's personal beliefs, was complete control of any land that ever fell into Jewish hands.[16] Indeed, Begin's 1978 declaration regarding the settlement of Neot Sinai,[17] as well as his announcement that 'there will be many more Elon Moreh',[18] expressed, to a great extent, his hawkish attitudes.

Following the May 1977 elections, Menachem Begin could lean on his close ideological partners and easily form a solid right-wing coalition that would have 63 seats. That would be a reflection of the voters' wishes: at the end of the day, Likud won the ballots in order to replace the old Mapai regime and to fulfil ideological promises, particularly regarding the major issues around which there were great divergences within Israeli society. Menachem Begin, however, took a different path. After decades of acting as the eternal militant opposition, he had become alienated from large segments of the public, and was well aware of it. Following the May 1977 electoral upheaval, he could do without Dash and its 15 seats; but beyond the mathematical results at the ballots, Begin was eager to win wide public support. Thus, Dash would soon become the party that would give the Likud leader the legitimacy he needed so badly in order to shake off his image of an extreme rightist.[19]

Additionally, Begin quite unexpectedly handed one of the most important ministerial portfolios, the Ministry of Foreign Affairs, to a dominant figure from the rival Labour party: Moshe Dayan.[20] With the Democratic Movement faction of the broken up Dash and Dayan at his side, Begin could now set sail on a new dovish political journey.

Phoenix parties: the National Religious Party

One of the great surprises of the 2013 elections was the emergence of a newly strengthened 12-seat national religious party.[21] After years of shrinking and constantly losing political power and usually gaining only five or six seats in the Knesset, and in recent campaigns falling as low as three seats, the national religious Habait Hayehudi (Jewish Home)[22] rose to 12 seats.[23] Naftali Bennett, who won the party's primaries shortly before the general elections with the slogan 'Something new is starting', represented a new national religious political actor: one who is nationalistic, but is also interested in the daily problems of the entire society; one who is religious, but his closest political aide is, by no coincidence, non-religious.[24] Bennett completed his military service as a special operations unit officer, like many other national religious young men in twenty-first century Israel, but is also a successful high-tech entrepreneur and businessman. Bennett wears a knitted yarmulke, but one does not need to look closely at it in order to realize that it is rather small.

The Mafdal (National Religious Party) merged several Zionist religious factions in 1956 to form one national religious bloc. The party's initial goal was to inspire a Jewish spirit within the framework of a Jewish democratic state; unlike the ultra-Orthodox streams, however, Mafdal never promoted the notion of theocracy (Halachic state) and strove to retain Israel's democratic character, along with active support of effective Jewish education and culture. Hence it was only natural that over the decades the party became the patron of the national religious school system, where Judaism is taught alongside mandatory educational subjects such as science, English and history. Mafdal also supports pre-military preparations for future Israel Defence Forces (IDF) draftees and Yeshivot Hesder, a programme where religious soldiers combine studying Torah with military combat service (though a shortened one).

As opposed to the ultra-Orthodox parties, which separate themselves from Israeli society, Mafdal always tried to live in both worlds: studying religion as well as joining the workforce; attending rabbinical colleges as well as serving in the military; praying in the synagogue as well as embracing modern culture. Perhaps one of the most prominent and genuine representatives of this attitude was the late Yosef Burg, who was one of the founders of the Mafdal and served for 40 years in the Knesset, partnering in almost every coalition and participating in governments led by either Labour or Likud. Burg viewed Mafdal as a bridge between the ultra-Orthodox and the secular, and between the left and right in Israeli politics. He had a habit of hyphenating the expression 'national-religious', and when he was asked which of the two elements was more important in the doctrine of his party, he quipped 'the hyphen'. This illustrates what President Shimon Peres said when Burg died in 1999: 'His most important legacy is that he tried to build a bridge over the biggest gulf in Israeli society, the gulf between religious and secular Jews; he was a religious man but he believed in compromise.'[25]

The 1967 War marked a historic change within Israel. The young national religious generation threw themselves wholeheartedly into building the new settlements in the post-1967 territories, thus placing the Zionist religious group on a well-defined side in the political controversy that was about to shake Israeli society during the coming decades. Consequently, Mafdal gradually ceased to be the ideological bridge between the left and the right, and slowly but surely turned into a distinctly right-wing party.

After having been a partner in every Labour government since the establishment of the state, it now became almost natural that with the 1977 political upheaval, Mafdal would break its historic alliance with Labour. The pragmatic moderation that was typical of this party turned into an extreme national ideology, particularly concerning the future of the territories. Radicalization on the political and diplomatic fronts was also accompanied by a partial turn toward religious extremism. Particularly after Zevulun Hammer's death, Mafdal leaders started to hand over veto powers to their rabbis, in total contradiction to the party's historic worldview, and allowed these rabbis to determine political policy.[26] A significant number of Mafdal voters felt uncomfortable with this turn of events and started voting for general non-sectoral parties, mainly the Likud.

The major result of the political and religious extremism was a split within the electorate: the Mafdal was separated into two or three different parties. The implementation of the peace process with Egypt during the early 1980s, as well as the Oslo process a decade later, gave rise to different factions that eventually competed with each other.[27]

When one understands fully the historical background of Mafdal, the 12 seats that Bennett gathered in the campaign are no longer a puzzle. It is not the story of a surprising new superstar, but the chronicle of the leadership returning to the party's ancient principles. A brief glance at the political platform of Bennett's haBayit HaYehudi party reveals that once the Jewish character of the state is mentioned, the love of country and people declared, and the importance of settling all the parts of the land is stressed, a long list of general issues follows. Here are some examples: (1) free market policies managed together with social solidarity; (2) equal opportunities encouraged by education; (3) an unbiased justice system and unbiased media; (4) the strengthening of the connections between Israel and Jewish communities all over the world; (5) supporting and aiding the disabled.

Mafdal's 2013 leader, who symbolically wears a tiny skullcap, is not a new phenomenon in national religious Zionism; his motto, 'Something new is starting', could actually be replaced by a different phrase, expressing the essence of his political success: 'the old Mafdal is back again'. Naftali Bennett owes his success to the traditional ideological compound that the party stood for during decades before it split in the 1980s. His success took place because he drove his political machine back into the past.

A sociological explanation

History, as we have seen, repeats itself. Even when one thinks that one has witnessed a totally new event, one is often largely witnessing repetition. Decades pass, people change, and the historic political episodes show striking similarities.

The sociological explanation for this phenomenon relies on the perception that groups provide definitions within society. Social groups serve as a primary source of personal values, and an important term that relates to this connection between the collective and the individual is *reference group*. The reference group is the social grouping with which a person relates, or aspires to relate, psychologically. The group becomes the frame of reference and the source for organizing one's experiences, perceptions and cognition. Reference groups are the standard for self-evaluation and form benchmarks for behaviour.[28] Noteworthy for our specific field of interest, reference groups have also proved to be a key factor in people's political preferences.[29] Sociology's group reference theory highly corresponds with *group identity* research conducted by political psychologists. During the last decade, collective identities based on race, ethnicity, religion, gender and other demographic traits have proved to be factors that generate political cohesion through a shared outlook and conformity to norms of political activity.[30] Among the collective partisan identities that play a central role in shaping the dynamics of public opinion, electoral choice and political behaviour, scholars count Republicans versus Democrats in the United States, Conservatives versus Labour supporters in the United Kingdom, and Social Democrats versus Christian Democrats in Germany. These are compared to the establishment of the Likud versus Labour electorates in Israel.[31]

Israeli society is marked by numerous diversities, and scholarly literature often presents four leading social divergences within the Jewish population of contemporary Israel:

(1) *Socio-economic divergence*: self-perception, as well as objective data that measure property ownership and consumer habits, indicate that Israeli society can be mainly defined as middle-class. Additionally, class consciousness is very weak; in the fairly economically homogeneous society, issues of inequality are mostly dismissed, although in practice wealth is very unequally distributed.

On the other hand, the absence of socio-economic tensions arises from manipulation by leading elites, who tend to divert attention away from social issues in order to increase the focus on security issues.[32]

(2) *Ethnic divergence*: one of the main Israeli social schisms is between the Jews of Middle Eastern background (Sephardim) and the Jews of European origins (Ashkenazim). This division splits the Israeli Jewish population into roughly two equal groups and encompasses almost all fields of life, with clear advantages for Ashkenazim over the Sephardim. Despite the empirical results of many studies which have shown that the socio-economic ethnic gap is narrowing in the second generation, studies that focused on university graduation rates and labour market earnings – arguably the two most important indicators of social standing in contemporary Israel – have indicated that the gaps are preserved over the generations.[33] A third ethnic group, the last decades' immigrants from Russia and Eastern Europe, who constitute more than 15% of the Israeli population, is commonly perceived as successfully integrating into the Ashkenazi middle class in Israel, despite the absorption difficulties they endured during transitional periods.[34]

(3) *Religious divergence:* religion versus modernity in the Jewish Israeli society is a complex issue. Generally speaking, however, when asked to define their attitudes towards religion, Israeli Jewish respondents tend to fall into the four classes: a little more than 50% perceive themselves as secular, about 20% as religious Zionists, approximately 20% as traditional, and roughly 10% as ultra-Orthodox.[35]

(4) *Political divergence*: the tension between right-wing and left-wing political perceptions has created a seesaw game in which political dominance has shifted from one side to the other.[36] Right-wing ideologies in Israel are closer to nationalism, with extreme rightists even justifying violent actions that might violate democratic principles;[37] in contrast, left-wing liberals tend to adopt a progressive and cosmopolitan viewpoint that goes along with secularism, equality and, above all, cultural tolerance. The major political dispute is between rightist advocates of settling the territories conquered in 1967 and leftist supporters of reconciliation, who encourage retreat and withdrawal for the sake of a peace process.[38]

The divergences within Israeli society have often been understood as overlapping. In his book titled *The End of Ashkenazi Hegemony,* sociologist Baruch Kimmerling coined the term 'Achusalim', the Hebrew acronym for Ashkenazi, secular, native (non-immigrant), partly socialist and partly nationalist Israelis. Kimmerling was referring to the elite groups of Israeli society, whose dominance he thought was reaching its end; the term he invented was comparable to the American term White Anglo-Saxon Protestants (WASPs). In Israel, Achusalim were the old established secular Zionists who had created the state, who controlled its economic structures and power institutes, ruled the academic and scientific establishments, the civil service and the army, who dictated cultural trends, ideological beliefs and, above all, engineered the precise Israeli prototype that the nation should identify with.[39]

Reference groups and collective identities go far beyond the framework of political parties, although partisan choice and collective identities nearly always overlap. The theory shows how historic recurrences of centrist middle-class parties are a representation of the Ashkenazi secular liberals, who, unlike Kimmerling's definition of the Achusalim, have neither socialist nor nationalistic tendencies. These are middle-class citizens whose social identities led them, more than once, to protest against the government. Being an elite group, they are confident that they will eventually end up having political leaders who will force the government to consider their protest.

The overlapping schisms/collective identities theory allows a perspective on the historic recurrence of a right-wing Likud leader who prefers left-wing rivals in his coalition because of his personal reference group. Until now, there has never been Israeli leadership that has not emerged from what Kimmerling defined as 'Achusalim', the reference group that dictates moderation and Western liberal attitudes. Even if he declares right-wing ideological principles, the elected Prime Minister will always restrain his policies, put them in a reasonable context, and recruit some of his rivals into government to create a situation where his hands are largely tied.

In the same manner, the sociological explanation for the re-emergence of the Mafdal would assume that about 10% of the Israeli population form the core electorate of the national religious party, which tends to rely on national values and is not extremist. Once Bennett and his proponents managed to form a religious Zionist block where both religious and national extremists were outnumbered and, to some extent, neutralized – his party obtained 12 seats, as the old Mafdal did four decades earlier.

The rational choice explanation

The other explanation that this paper offers for the phenomenon of historic recurrence relies on theories of rational choice based on comparative studies. Political circumstances constantly change and challenge parties. New demands are made, new issues are introduced, and new popular preferences are raised. Party-political principles are expected to follow and change as well. Electoral competition may lead to constant and smooth adaptation of parties' preferences.[40] It seems, then, that the Israeli political system, just like any other of its kind, would always be in constant change.

Parties' change of policies may also occur once they see elections as competitive and when they need extra votes in order to win. However, if winning or losing is perceived as certain, parties would not need to make efforts to win further votes or adapt their programme.[41] Once any party can rely on solid support among the electorate – no change in any of these parties will be seen in the long run.

Since parties have imperfect information at best about their chances at the ballots, and since they have no knowledge about the median voter's position, ideologically and politically they tend to move little, or not at all; in this way, they have a better chance to retain the votes they already have. Thus, ideological stagnation, or at least a barely changing set of principles, is expected to characterize every political system.[42] Empirical research tends to confirm this argument, and to show long-term stability in party preferences. Although parties' programmed left–right positions, for example, do alter, major changes are very uncommon. Party ideology is rigid and the party may be characterized to a great measure by lack of responsiveness to either external problems or electoral concerns.[43] This may partially explain how, after decades of democratic campaigns, we still find the very same ideological principles in different political platforms.

These findings about the rigidity of political actors fit well with the assertion that political institutions in general are limited in their ability to respond to external stimuli. Due to cognitive and institutional limitations, political institutions hardly react proportionally to signals that may reach them from their surroundings. Scholars claim that institutions tend to neglect these signals altogether, and either do not change at all, or tend to overreact and change dramatically, much more than was demanded for by external signals. Although incentives from the outside world do enter the system, they are filtered and ignored. Consequently, policies slowly drift away from reality. They lose their capability to deal with real-world problems and are no longer familiar with popular preferences. Policies are confined to small groups of decision makers with a monopoly and are detached from matters outside the closed circle of policy insiders.[44] Opponents of each of the parties that we have reviewed in this paper (Yesh Atid, Mafdal, Likud), as well as adversaries of several other parties, would embrace these findings and claim that this proves how their political rivals are ideologically outdated.

Since policies hardly change and become increasingly irrelevant to the changing reality, accidents are bound to happen. Wars, revolutions or even gradual evolutionary events suddenly reveal the inadequacy of the ongoing policy. This is when dramatic and sudden policy shifts happen. The political institution at stake engages in a kind of catch-up operation and tries to devise a fundamentally new policy to deal with the changed situation. Policy monopolies are broken down, and new policy monopolies emerge. This process of lagging behind and catching up is considered by scholars to characterize, for example, all political institutions in the United States.[45]

Political institutions, political parties included, have severe cognitive and institutional limitations that result in lagging behind reality and then catching up in bursts. The cognitive architecture of institutions only allows them to deal with one important problem at a time. Organizations suffer from an inevitable bottleneck. Dealing with normal issues, most of the time, organizations can rely on parallel processing. But when genuinely important matters appear, the organization's leadership has to devote a significant amount of attention to it. Since the resources of time and energy of decision makers are limited, the tendency is to neglect most issues most of the time. Political leaders try to manage their scarce time while constantly juggling issues, checking whether anything has changed and, if not, confirming previous decisions and stances.[46]

Israel is probably not so different, in this sense, from the American example. The crisis gives birth to new formations – such as a centrist new political party, as we have seen; but the system will eventually strive to return to stability. There is, therefore, a great probability that the new party will decline, though not necessarily as dramatically as Dash, who after the great success of 1977 fell apart and did not even participate as a party in the following 1981 elections. This may be the situation until the next opportunity for a similar party emerges, as was the case after the 2011 summer protests that gave birth to Yesh Atid in the 2013 elections.

The cognitive limits of political parties and their leaders reduce their reaction to incoming signals. Parties are unable to attend to every piece of information available in the outside world. They ignore signals all the time and are forced to catch up later when it turns out that these overlooked signals were important. Since ideology is the *raison d'être* of every party, parties tend to devote more attention to issues that can easily be linked with and framed within their ideology, and tend to disregard other issues. Thus, not only does their ideology restrict the scope of their attention and the issues they regularly monitor, but their ideology also severely limits their capacity to react. Additionally, parties are identified by the outside world with particular issues. In fact, parties have to offer choices to the electorate – that is part of their function in a democracy. To be able to offer choices, they must differ, and to differ they must hold on to their ideology.

Only by offering stable choices to the electorate can an inattentive and superficially informed electorate make reasonably correct choices. If parties constantly adjusted their stance, voters would be confused; they would not be able to single out the party that roughly corresponds to their beliefs. Hence, even if parties wanted to betray their past and fundamentally change their stances or issue attention, their voters would probably not believe them.[47]

Conclusion

Notwithstanding this article's pronounced goal to illuminate the phenomenon of historical recurrences in Israeli politics, we are bound to be left with several options, none of which can solidly be proved as the most effective. Which of the theories – either the sociological one or those taken from political science – gives the best explanation remains unclear. Both sets of explanations analyse reality with different academic tools, each of them revealing the characteristics of the Israeli political system from a different angle. Reference groups and collective identities are a key factor in the sociological behaviour of voters and their political leaders; the rules of rational choice are probably just as important for any attempt to comprehend the way parties, voters and their elected politicians act.

One thing, however, remains certain: during the next rounds of democratic elections we expect to witness surprising events. We expect to encounter centrist blocs, old and defeated parties that come back to life and gain the very same electorate they had lost, and elected right-wing nationalistic prime ministers who shift to moderation and liberalism the moment their campaign is over, or, correspondingly, left-wing prime ministers whose liberalism becomes somewhat restrained once they enter office.

Disclosure statement

No potential conflict of interest was reported by the author.

Notes on contributor

Eyal Lewin is assistant professor in the Department of Middle Eastern Studies and Political Science at Ariel University, and a research fellow at the Dan Shomron Kinneret Centre for Peace, Security and Society.

Notes

1. Dominic Lieven, *Russia Against Napoleon: The True Story of the Campaigns of War and Peace* (New York: Viking, 2011), 417–542.
2. David M. Glanz, *Barbarossa: Hitler's Invasion of Russia, 1941* (Stroud: Tempus, 2001); David M. Glanz and Jonathan M. House, *When Titans Clashed: How the Red Army Stopped Hitler* (Lawrence, KS: University Press of Kansas, 1995); Louis Rotundo, "The Creation of Soviet Reserves and the 1941 Campaign," *Military Affairs* 50, no. 1 (1986): 21–8.

3. Barbara W. Tuchman, *The Zimmerman Telegram* (New York: Ballantine Books, 1958), 168–83.
4. Alistair Horne, *A Savage War of Peace: Algeria 1954–1962* (New York: New York Review Books, 1977), 273–534.
5. See *Yediot Ahronoth*, January 23, 2013.
6. See *Ma'ariv*, January 23, 2013.
7. See the political platform of *Yesh Atid* on the party's website: http://yeshatid.org.il/wp-content/uploads/2013/02/yeshatid_platform.pdf
8. Ecclesiastes 1:9, King James Bible version.
9. Abraham Diskin, *The Last Days in Israel: Understanding the New Israeli Democracy* (London: Frank Cass, 2003), 55–67.
10. See the political platform of Shinui in the website archive of the IDI (Israel Democracy Institute): http://www.idi.org.il/media/393952/shinuy%209.pdf
11. Jonathan Mendilow, *Ideology, Party Change and Electoral Campaigns in Israel, 1965–2001* (Albany, NY: SUNY, 2003), 39–64; Rafael Medoff and Chaim Waxman, *Historical Dictionary of Zionism* (New York: Routledge, 2000), 61–3; Moshe Lissak, *The Elites of the Jewish Community in Palestine* [in Hebrew] (Tel Aviv, Israel: Am Oved, 1981), 162–7; Binyamin Neuberger, *Government and Politics – the Parties in Israel* [in Hebrew] (Tel Aviv: Open University, 1997), 95–102; Yaniv Ben Uzi, "Let Us Live Here in This Country! The General Zionist Party, 1949–1952" [in Hebrew], *Kathedra* 127 (2008): 141–68.
12. Asaf Carmel, "Journalist and Outspoken Former Justice Minister Yosef Lapid Dies Aged 77," *Ha'aretz*, June 2, 2008.
13. Samuel Willard Crompton, *Ariel Sharon* (New York: Infobase Publishing, 2007), 48–55, 94–9.
14. For a full review of the connection between the two parties during the 1980s and 1990s see Arye Dayan, *The Story of Shas* (Jerusalem: Keter, 1998). For accounts of the demographic and ideological closeness of the potential voters of the two parties see Asher Arian and Michal Shamir, eds., *The Elections in Israel – 1984* (New Brunswick, NJ: Transaction Books, 1986); Asher Arian and Michal Shamir, eds., *The Elections in Israel – 1988* (Boulder, CO: Westview Press, 1990); Asher Arian and Michal Shamir, eds., *The Elections in Israel – 1992* (Albany, NY: SUNY, 1995); Asher Arian and Michal Shamir, eds., *The Elections in Israel – 1996* (Albany, NY: SUNY, 1999); Asher Arian and Michal Shamir, eds., *The Elections in Israel – 1999* (Albany, NY: SUNY, 2002); Asher Arian and Michal Shamir, eds., *The Elections in Israel – 2001* (Jerusalem: Israel Democracy Institute, 2002); Asher Arian and Michal Shamir, eds., *The Elections in Israel – 2003* (New Brunswick, NJ: Transaction Books, 2005); Asher Arian and Michal Shamir, eds., *The Elections in Israel – 2006* (New Brunswick, NJ: Transaction Books, 2008); Asher Arian and Michal Shamir, eds., *The Elections in Israel – 2009* (New Brunswick, NJ: Transaction Books, 2010).
15. A basic coalition of 61 seats could be made by Likud–Israel Beitenu – 31 seats; Jewish Home – 12 seats; Shas – 11 seats; United Torah Judaism – seven seats.
16. Neta Oren, *The Israeli Ethos of Conflict 1967–2006* (Arlington, VA: George Mason University, 2009).
17. Neot Sinai was a Herut-affiliated settlement in the north-eastern part of the Sinai Peninsula, and Begin's declaration was immediately equated to Ben Gurion's 1953 decision to make Sde Boker, in the desert, his retirement home and keeping his membership in that Kibbutz even when he returned to office.
18. Elon Moreh was a settlement in Samaria that was evicted again and again on legal grounds ever since 1974. The struggle became a symbolic one and before certain concessions were made about the exact location of the settlement Begin gave this well-known declaration. See Begin's exact declaration concerning some of its

impacts in Arnon Lamprom, ed., *Chaim Herzog The Sixth President: Documentation, 1918–1997* (Jerusalem, Israel: State Archive, 2009), 348.

19. Diskin, *The Last Days in Israel*, 55–67.

20. Once Dayan accepted Begin's offer and joined his government, he was expelled from the Labour party. Two years later he resigned his post because of disagreements with Begin concerning the Palestinian issue. See Yael Dayan, *My Father, His Daughter* (New York: Farrar, Straus & Giroux, 1985), 174–85.

21. Several newspapers crowned Naftali Bennett as the great surprise of the election campaign. See for example correspondent Harriet Sherwood, who referred to Bennett as 'the surprise star' in an interview with him in the *Guardian*, January 7, 2013; correspondent Ari Shavit, who called Bennett 'the big surprise' in an interview with him in *Ha'aretz*, December 28, 2012; Likud MK Danny Danon, who in an interview by Robert Tait calls the Jewish Home 'the surprise package' in the *Telegraph*, January 20, 2013.

22. The Jewish Home, Habait Hayehudi, will be referred to henceforth as Mafdal, using the name of the historic party from which it originally emerged.

23. The chronology of Mafdal electoral achievements: from 1957 to 1977 – 10–12 seats in each campaign; 1981 – six seats; 1984 – four seats; 1988 – five seats; 1992 – six seats; 1996 – nine seats; 1999 – five seats; 2003 – six seats; 2006 – three seats; 2009 – three seats; 2013 – 12 seats.

24. Ayelet Shaked, a self-declared secularist who became the first secular MK of a religious party.

25. The quotations are taken from the reports about his death and burial ceremonies in *Los Angeles Times*, October 16, 1999.

26. Gerald Steinberg, "Take the Rabbis Out of Politics," *Jerusalem Post*, July 3, 1998.

27. For a full account of the entire process see Yehuda Ben Meir, *The Rise and Fall of the Mafdal* [in Hebrew] (Jerusalem: Israel Democracy Institute, 2008); Ofer Kenig, *Farewell to Mafdal* [in Hebrew] (Jerusalem: Israel Democracy Institute, 2008); Nadav Perry, "Naftali Bennett Brings New Start for Israel's National Religious Party," *Al-Monitor*, January 20, 2013. Cited in: http://www.al-monitor.com/pulse/tr/contents/ articles/opinion/2013/05/a-new-beginning-for-the-national-religious-party.html#

28. Pamela Johnston Conover and Stanley Feldman, "Group Identification, Values and the Nature of Political Beliefs," *American Politics Quarterly* 12 (1984): 151–75; Ann B. Bettencourt and Deborah Hume, "The Cognitive Contents of Social Group Identity: Values, Emotions, and Relationships," *Journal of Social Psychology* 29 (1999): 113–21; Patrick C.L. Heaven, "Group Identities and Human Values," *Journal of Social Psychology* 139 (1999): 190–95.

29. Geoffrey L. Cohen, "Party Over Policy: The Dominating Impact of Group Influence on Political Beliefs," *Journal of Personality and Social Psychology* 85, no. 5 (2003): 808–22.

30. Michael S. Lewis-Beck, William G. Jacoby, Helmut Norpoth, and Herbert F. Weisberg, *The American Voter Revisited* (Ann Arbor, MI: University of Michigan Press, 2008); Bernd Simon and Bert Klandermans, "Politicized Collective Identity: A Social Psychological Analysis," *American Psychologist* 56 (2001): 319–31.

31. Leonie Huddy, "From Group Identity to Political Cohesion and Commitment," in *Oxford Handbook of Political Psychology*, ed. Leonie Huddy, David O. Sears, and Jack Levy (New York: Oxford University Press, 2013), 511–43.

32. Dan Horowitz and Moshe Lissak, *Trouble in Utopia: The Overburden Polity of Israel* (Albany, NY: SUNY, 1989); Sammy Smooha, *Arabs and Jews in Israel, Vol. 2: Change and Continuity in Mutual Intolerance* (Boulder, CO: Westview Press, 1992); Sammy Smooha, "Class, Ethnic and National Cleavages and Democracy in Israel," in *Israeli Democracy under Stress*, ed. Ehud Sprinzak and L. Diamond (Boulder, CO: Lynne Rienner Publishers, 1993).

33. Yinon Cohen and Yitzhak Haberfeld, "Second-Generation Jewish Immigrants in Israel: Have the Ethnic Gaps in Schooling and Earnings Declined?," *Ethnic and Racial Studies* 21, no. 3 (1998): 507–28.

34. Majid Al-Haj and Eli Leshem, *Immigrants from the Former Soviet Union in Israel – Ten Years Later: A Research Report* (Haifa: University of Haifa, Center for Multiculturalism and Educational Research, 2000); Moshe Lissak and Eli Leshem, "The Russian Intelligentsia in Israel: Between Ghettoization and Integration," *Israel Affairs* 2, no. 2 (2000): 20–36.

35. Eliezer Ben-Rafael, "The Faces of Religiosity in Israel: Cleavages or Continuum?," *Israel Studies* 6 (2008): 94–120; Daniel J. Elazar, "The 1981 Elections: Into the Second Generation of Statehood," in *Israel at the Polls, 1981*, ed. Howard R. Penniman and Daniel J. Elazar (Washington, DC: Indiana University Press, 1986).

36. Eran Kaplan, *The Jewish Radical Right* (Madison, WI: University of Wisconsin Press, 2005).

37. Daphna Canetti-Nisim, Eran Zaidise, and Ami Pedahzur, "Militant Attitudes among Israelis throughout the al-Aqsa Intifada," *Palestine–Israel Journal of Politics, Economics and Culture* 11, no. 3/4 (2005): 104–11.

38. Michal Shamir and Asher Arian, "Collective Identity and Electoral Competition in Israel," *American Political Science Review* 93, no. 2 (1999): 265–77.

39. Baruch Kimmerling, *The End of Ashkenazi Hegemony* [in Hebrew] (Jerusalem: Keter Publishing House Ltd, 2001).

40. This argument was established by Downs. See Anthony Downs, *An Economic Theory of Democracy* (New York: Harper & Row, 1957). Arguments of rational choice theories have also been validated by studies based on work of the Manifesto Research Group that collected data about the dynamics of partisan political principles in 25 different countries over a period of 50 years. The time-span of the study was 1945–1998. The 25 countries are all Western democracies complemented with the United States, Australia, New Zealand, Canada, Japan, Turkey and Israel. The total number of parties covered in the dataset is 288, and it covers 364 different national elections. For a full account of the Manifesto Research Group's data collection see Ian Budge and Hans-Dieter Klingemann, "Finally! Comparative Over-Time Mapping of Party Policy Movement," in *Mapping Policy Preferences: Estimates for Parties, Electors and Governments 1945–1998*, eds. Ian Budge et al. (Oxford: Oxford University Press, 2001), 19–50.

41. David Robertson, *A Theory of Party Competition* (New York: Wiley, 1976).

42. Ian Budge, "A New Spatial Theory of Party Competition: Uncertainty, Ideology and Policy Equilibria Viewed Comparatively and Spatially," *British Journal of Political Science* 24, no. 4 (1994): 443–67.

43. Ian Budge and Judith Bara, "Manifesto-Based Research: A Critical Overview," in *Mapping Policy Preferences* (see note 40), 51–73.

44. Frank R. Baumgartner and Bryan D. Jones, *Agendas and Instability in American Politics* (Chicago, IL: University of Chicago Press, 1993); Bryan Jones and Frank Baumgartner, *The Politics of Attention. How Government Prioritizes Attention* (Chicago, IL: University of Chicago Press, 2005).

45. Bryan D. Jones, Tracy Sulkin, and Heather A. Larsen, "Policy Punctuations in American Political Institutions," *American Political Science Review*, 97, 1 (2003): 151–69.

46. Jones and Baumgartner, *The Politics of Attention. How Government Prioritizes Attention*.

47. Hans-Dieter Klingemann, Robert Hofferbert, and Ian Budge, *Parties, Policies and Democracy* (Oxford: Westview, 1994); Michael McDonald, Ian Budge, and Paul Pennings, "Choice versus Sensitivity: Party Reactions to Public Concerns," *European Journal of Political Research* 43, no. 6 (2004): 845–68.

Index

References to tables are in **bold**.

Abbas, Mahmoud 6, 9
Achusalim (term) 81, 126
Alcorn, Marshall W. 104
Aloni, Shulamit 90
Am Shalem party 60
Amossy, Ruth 105
Amsalem, Rabbi Haim 55, 60, 61, 64
Arab Balad 3
Ariel, Uri 26, 43
Aristotle 104
Attias, Ariel 59–60
Auerbach, Rabbi Shmuel 58, 59
Aviner, Rabbi Shlomo 40
Ayalon, Danny 4

Balad 6
Bang, Henrik 112
Bank Hapaolim 91–2
Barak, Ehud 3, 4, 5, 10
Barnea, Nahum 119
Bayit Yedhudi 65
Begin, Menachem 121–2
Beitar Ilit 65
Beiteinu party: Russian-Israeli support for 69, 70, 71–3, 79, 81–2; *see also* Likud/ Beiteinu alliance
Bennett, Naftali: election as chairman of Habayit Hayehudi 3, 42; election results 13; order to expel Jews controversy 6, 7; personal attacks on 7, 9, 47–8; personal biography 45; public image of 44, 45; and settler interests 26–7; 2013 election campaign 31, 34, 42, 43–4; 2013 election primaries 3, 41–2; use of social media 45, 106, 107, 108, 109; *see also* Habayit Hayehudi

Boorstin, Daniel 88
Bourdieu, Pierre 86–7, 88–9, 95
Breslov Hassidim 65
Brinton, Alan 104
Burg, Yosef 123

celebrities: celebrity status of Lapid, Yair 86–7, 91–2, 96; definition of 88; in Israeli politics, 1950-60s 89–90; media capital 86–7; social capital 86; symbolic capital 86
centre-left parties: campaign tactics 25; centre-left mega party 1–2, 9–10; effects of far-right ideologies 25; and middle-class appeal 118–20; voters' socio-demographic traits 28; *see also* Habayit Hayehudi; Yesh Atid
Chabad Hassidim 65

Danon, Danny 4
Dash party 90, 119–20, 122, 128
Davis, Aeron 86–7, 89, 94–5
Dayan, Moshe 89, 122
Deri, Aryeh 2–3, 8, 9, 59–60
Dichter, Avi 4
Disengagement Plan 34, 35–6

economics: budget deficit 11–12; tax rises 8; 2011 social protests 65–6, 80–1, 101–2, 118–19
Edelstein, Yuri 8
Egypt 6, 8
18th Knesset 1
el-Erian, Essam 8
Elkin, Zeev 8